Ghosthunting
ILLINOIS

AMERICA'S
HAUNTED
ROADTRIP

Ghosthunting
ILLINOIS

JOHN B. KACHUBA

Published by Clerisy Press
Distributed by Publishers Group West
Printed in the United States of America
First edition, third printing

Cover and interior photos provided by John B. Kachuba, with the following exceptions: pps. 30, 32 courtesy of the Chicago Public Library, p. 190 courtesy of Jon Musgrave

Library of Congress Cataloging-in-Publication Data
     Kachuba, John B., 1950–
          Ghosthunting Illinois / John B. Kachuba.
               p. cm. — (The haunted heartland series)
          Includes bibliographical references.

     ISBN-13: 978-1-57860-220-9
     ISBN-10: 1-57860-220-3
          1. Haunted places—Illinois. 2. Ghosts—Illinois. I. Title. II. Series.

     BF1472.U6K32 2005
     133.1'09773--dc22
                                             2005012050

Editor: Jack Heffron
Cover Design: Kelly N. Kofron
Interior Design: Carie Reeves

Clerisy Press
1700 Madison Road
Cincinnati, Ohio 45206
www.clerisypress.com

For Riley Elizabeth

CONTENTS

Ghosthunting
Travel Guide

ABOUT THE AUTHOR

John B. Kachuba is the author of *Ghosthunting Ohio, How to Write Funny,* and (with his wife, Mary A. Newman, PhD) *Why Is This Job Killing Me?* His short fiction and nonfiction have been widely published. He is a recent winner of the Dogwood Fiction Prize and has been published in such journals as *Tin House, Hawaii Pacific Review, Connecticut Review, Mississippi Quarterly,* and others. He holds advanced degrees in creative writing from Antioch University and Ohio University. He currently lives in Athens, Ohio.

Introduction

WHY IS IT WE MORTALS ARE TERRIFIED BY THE prospect of encountering ghosts and yet so many of us harbor a fascination and yearning for just such a meeting? Why do so many of us share this morbid obsession with ghosts? As children we read ghost stories under the bedcovers at night or huddled around a campfire, afraid to look over our shoulders, as someone told us a ghost story. Some of us grew up near old, abandoned houses that we were certain were haunted, houses that simultaneously repelled and attracted us. We learned, almost instinctively, that we had no business being in cemeteries after nightfall. We learned to whistle in the dark.

One explanation for such an intense interest in ghosts and the world of the paranormal may be a simple one: our fear of death, of life simply coming to an end. If ghosts do exist, then we can be assured that there is some existence for us beyond the grave. Many theologies presuppose an eternal existence after death, often connected to concepts of reward or punishment based upon the lives we led here on earth. These theologies provide comfort for their adherents, but some lingering doubt often remains. After all, has anyone returned from Heaven—or Hell for that matter—to tell us what those places are like?

But then there are ghosts, creatures once living, now dead who exist on a plane somewhere between these eternal realms and that of the living. It is the ghosts who appear to us, speak to us, and let us know that existence in some form goes on. Death is not the ultimate destination of the living, they tell us, but only a transfer station of sorts to somewhere else. Ghosts connect us in varied ways to a future we cannot comprehend and to a past we may have known little about. There are many stories of ghosts of deceased family members appearing to living relatives to offer comfort or advice in difficult times. There are also as many stories about ghosts who are able to help shed light on past mysteries or injustices, such as unsolved crimes. It may be these connections that stoke our interest in ghosts.

In 2003, I set out to explore this fascination with ghosts. I traveled throughout my home state of Ohio, visiting more than thirty haunted locations. My experiences were published the following year as *Ghosthunting Ohio*. But far from answering my questions about ghosts, my experiences led to more questions and my interest was piqued. I decided to extend my ghosthunting experiences and *Ghosthunting Illinois*, the second in the Haunted Heartland series, is the result.

Throughout much of 2004–2005, I roamed Illinois, checking out almost forty haunted locations. I started off with a lengthy list of haunted locations drawn from many different sources. The Internet sites of various ghost groups, as well as books written by other writers, gave me some ideas for places to visit. The Internet, of course, can lead you down many interesting paths. I would never have guessed that there was actually a Museum of Funeral Customs, or that it was in Illinois, right outside the gates of Springfield's Oak Ridge Cemetery, where Abraham Lincoln is buried, had my wife, Mary, not discovered it while doing some research on the Web.

Some of the places were found not so much as a result of research as much as from a stroke of dumb luck, maybe a hunch. As Mary and I passed by an old bed-and-breakfast in a small Illinois town, Mary said she thought the place was probably haunted. I stopped at the house and spoke with the owner, who admitted the house was haunted but didn't want it written about in the book. A similar hunch of hers, however, resulted in the chapter about the C. H. Moore Homestead. You just never know.

Each of the places in the book is open to the public and is part of an eclectic list of haunted theatres, churches, restaurants and bars, hotels, historic sites, cemeteries, museums, and libraries. Mary accompanied me on several of these ramblings, so we were able to trade notes and compare our experiences. I went to each of these places with an open mind and no preconceived notions about the existence of ghosts. I had read too many books about hauntings from writers who see ghosts on every street corner and, frankly, I find such books unbelievable. I am not a "sensitive," "psychic," or "medium." In fact, I'm an extra-large. I'm an average person, just like you, with a curiosity about things paranormal. My intentions as I wrote this book were to accurately and objectively describe for you my observations and experiences, as well as the experiences of others I met along the way, and then let you draw your own conclusions about ghosts and hauntings.

I encourage you to visit these places and explore them for yourself. Some may require calling ahead for appointments; others may be open only on certain days during the week. Check the "Visiting Haunted Sites" section in the back of this book for complete information. In addition to addresses and phone numbers, the section also gives you their Web address and hours of operation if available for each location as well as important travel tips.

Having visited close to sixty haunted sites over the last two years, I've developed some guidelines for ghosthunting that I think you may find useful in your own research:

1. **Conduct all your investigations with an open mind, but don't let yourself be fooled by the "evidence."** No one has yet been able to scientifically prove or disprove the existence of ghosts, and it's unlikely you will be the one to earn that fame. Better simply to be non-judgmental and open to whatever you experience and observe for yourself. Be hard-nosed about the "evidence" you uncover. Make certain that you exhaust all possible explanations before you claim a brush with the supernatural.

2. **Interview witnesses separately.** Take a page from standard police procedures and always talk to witnesses of paranormal phenomena separately so that one witness's testimony does not influence that of another. It's easy for people in a group to "remember" things they never actually saw, making it difficult for the researcher to sort out fact from fiction.

3. **Document your activities.** I always carry a notebook and pen, tape recorder, and camera with me when investigating a site. The tape recorder is used to interview witnesses, but some people have also used it to record background sound over a period of time to try to catch unidentifiable sounds or voices of the dead

in a particular location, a phenomenon known as electronic voice phenomena (EVP).

A note about photography as documentation is important here. Many people, using either traditional cameras or digital cameras, have reported various anomalies on the photos once they are developed or downloaded onto a computer. These anomalies, usually whitish orbs but also misty smears and other amorphous shapes, are invisible to the naked eye when the photo is taken. There are many reasonable explanations for these objects. They may be dust particles or water droplets on the camera lens. They may be reflections caused by the flash of other cameras or by common objects—even some insects reflecting the camera flash—which the photographer simply did not notice at the time. Your finger, or the camera strap covering part of the camera lens, may also be possible explanations for your photogenic ghost. Enlarging the photo will often help you identify the anomaly accurately. Despite all these reasonable explanations, there are hundreds of "ghost photos" that defy explanation—much to my surprise, I have taken some myself while writing this book. Still, it is important not to jump to conclusions when these anomalies show up. Rule out all logical explanations first before deciding you've captured a ghost on film.

4. **Respect the site.** It is important to remember that any haunted site carries with it a history of both the people that inhabited the site and of the site itself. That history is worthy of your respect. You should observe whatever rules and regulations might be in effect for the site and work within them. In other words, you should not be breaking into buildings or removing anything from them as souvenirs. Nor should you be prowling around cemeteries after posted hours. You will find people more receptive to helping you with your explorations if you follow the rules.

5. **Respect the privacy of your contacts.** Some people may tell you their ghost stories, but for a variety of reasons, may not want other people to know their identity. You must respect their

right to privacy. Unless noted otherwise, all the names of the persons appearing in this book are their real names. I told all my contacts that I was writing a book and asked for permission to use their real names. If permission was not granted—which was rare—or if I was unable to obtain a name for some reason, I told their stories using pseudonyms. These pseudonyms are identified in the text by an (*) after the name.

6. **Be a knowledgeable ghosthunter.** This last point is perhaps the most important one. No one really knows the rules and laws of the spirit world. Ghosthunters are always exploring terra incognita and finding their way by learning from others, but it is important to learn from those who are serious about their work rather than from people who are merely looking for kicks. Knowledge about ghosts and the spirit world will increase your chances of obtaining your goals, but more importantly, will keep you safe. But you should also be knowledgeable about the real world as well. Know the geography and history of the place you are visiting before you go. Is it a desolate location? How safe is it, both structurally and in terms of its environment? A Spiritualist minister I met along the way told me that she "fears the living more than the dead." While I do not want to sound like an alarmist, I do believe a little bit of caution and common sense can go a long way toward making your ghosthunting experience safe and fun.

I hope you find *Ghosthunting Illinois* enjoyable and helpful to you. As always, I am curious about your experiences and would love to hear from you. Feel free to drop me a line through my Web site at www.johnkachuba.com and also watch for my new book, *Ghosthunters*, to be published in 2006.

Happy ghosthunting!

John B. Kachuba
Athens, Ohio

Metro Chicago

Metro Chicago (COOK COUNTY)
Beverly Unitarian Church
Biograph Theater
Ghosts of the *Eastland*
Glessner House
Graceland Cemetery
Jane Addams Hull-House Museum
Museum of Science and Industry
Red Lion Pub

Beverly Unitarian Church

CHICAGO

THERE IS AN INTERESTING DEBATE AMONG PEOPLE
of faith about whether ghosts exist or not and if a belief in ghosts can
be reconciled with a belief in some religious creed. Every religion has
stories of supernatural beings, creatures that exist in another realm
that is invisible and unknown to mere mortals. We have various
names for such beings, depending upon our own cultural beliefs—
angels, spirits, demons, guides—but what they all have in common
is that they are non-flesh-and-blood beings that have various forms of
interaction with humans. The beings themselves were never human
and are considered as purely spiritual creatures. Ghosts, on the other
hand, are distinct from these entities in that they were, at one time,
human beings with the same wants and desires, pains and sorrows,

joys and successes that are all indicative of the human experience. It is this difference between once-human and never-human, eternally spiritual and formerly mortal that fuels the debate.

For the members of the Beverly Unitarian Church on Chicago's South Side, the debate is of little consequence. One of the seven principles of the Unitarian Universalist Association, of which the Beverly church is a member, supports "a free and responsible search for truth and meaning," a concept that allows for both a belief in ghosts as well as a disbelief. The choice is left up to the individual and is not dictated by some religious hierarchy.

It came as no surprise to me then to find that the Beverly Unitarian Church was haunted.

My wife, Mary, and I were familiar with the Unitarian Universalist church, having attended services in our hometown of Athens, Ohio, so we decided to go to the Sunday service at Beverly while we were in Chicago researching this book. The fact that the church was haunted was an added incentive, of course. It was a warm and sunny day in August when we pulled into the parking lot adjacent to an imposing building that looked like a castle, and was in fact nicknamed "the Irish Castle" by its neighbors.

The castle sat on a little hill at the corner of 103rd Street and Longwood Drive in a quiet residential neighborhood. The three-story limestone block structure was built in 1886 by wealthy real estate magnate Robert C. Givens and modeled after a castle he saw while traveling in Ireland. Givens and his family lived in the house only a few years before selling it. The building then served as a private residence for various people and, at one point, housed the Chicago Female College. In 1942, it became the home of the Unitarian Fellowship.

Mary and I were early. No one else had arrived and the door was locked, so we walked around to the front of the building. Rounded corner towers rose above the trees. The crenellated battlements and the massive Romanesque arch above the solid-wood door called to mind images of King Arthur, or maybe the moody Dane, Hamlet, chatting with the ghost of his father on a cold and moonless night. Ivy crept along the stone steps leading up to the castle and twined around the towers. Unlike a real medieval castle, this one featured many large windows.

After a few minutes, people began to arrive for the services, so we followed them inside. Those large windows admitted plenty of light and the interior was bright and airy, not at all what one would expect inside a castle. We spoke with some of the people as they entered and were invited to tour the building before the service began. The ground level, now used as the main worship space, was one large room at the front of the house and had originally been the parlor. A large piano stood before the windows.

A beautifully carved oak staircase led up to the second floor. This floor, too, was essentially one large room, with a kitchen on one side. I didn't know for sure, but my guess was that many of the original interior walls on both floors had been removed in order to open up the interior and create larger spaces. On this floor, as on the ground floor, the rounded corner towers created cozy little nooks, some of them furnished with chairs. Another stairway led to the third-floor apartment of the caretaker, who was not at home the day we visited.

It is not uncommon for Unitarian services to be conducted without a minister, led instead by one of the members of the fellowship. We joined the others downstairs and listened as one of the members of the fellowship talked about his struggle with depression. Halfway through his talk, I heard a thump on the ceiling above me. It didn't quite register with me until it sounded again, and I remembered that we had been the last ones upstairs. There was nobody up there now.

"Did you hear that?" I whispered, leaning toward Mary.

She nodded.

"What do you think it was?"

"I don't know," she said.

I listened carefully, but the sound did not return.

The service concluded and we found ourselves chatting with the woman who had been sitting next to us. Pat Haynes, a longtime member of the fellowship, was happy to talk to us about the castle ghost.

"No one is really sure who she is," Pat said. "People have seen a young woman dressed in white, something like a nightgown. Some say she is the ghost of a girl named Clara, one of the students here when this place was the women's college. They say she died in the 1930s from influenza."

I wondered if a young female ghost from a women's college would be so rude as to clump around upstairs and make the thumping sounds I had heard.

"Have you ever seen her?" Mary asked.

"No," Pat said, "but some of the old-timers have. There's another theory," Pat continued, "that she may be the ghost of Eleanor Veil, a woman who lived here during the Depression."

Although I was carefully listening to what Pat was saying, I was distracted by the glass jar she held in her hands. "Can I ask you what you've got in that jar?" I finally said.

"Oh, this?" She laughed and held up the jar so I could see inside it. There were a few green leaves and some fuzzy little, I don't know ...things.

"What am I looking at?"

"These are monarch butterfly caterpillars," Pat said, "and the leaves are milkweed. That's the only thing the caterpillars will eat."

I wondered why she had brought the caterpillars to church, but before I could ask her, she said, "You should talk to Fran Johnson. I'm sure she's got a ghost story for you."

No sooner had Pat spoken her name than Fran came over to us. Mary and I recognized her as someone we had spoken to earlier, although we didn't get her name the first time.

"Are you talking about me?" Fran said, with a smile.

"They're interested in ghost stories about this place, and I told them you might have one for them," Pat said.

Fran looked at me quizzically.

"I'm writing a book," I said.

Experience had already taught me that most people, contrary to what I would have expected, would pour out their hearts to me once I told them I was writing a book. Maybe they felt sorry for me, or maybe I was just cheaper than a therapist. In any case, Fran was willing to talk.

"It was during an evening meeting of the Ladies of the Castle,"

Fran said. "We were meeting upstairs on the second floor. Since there was no one else in the building except our group, the lights were off down here on the first floor."

As the ladies were talking, they heard faint tinkling sounds from downstairs. The sounds grew louder and became recognizable as someone playing the piano.

"There wasn't supposed to be anyone down there, so I went downstairs to check it out," Fran said. "I could hear the piano clearly. I threw on the lights and the sounds stopped, but there was no one there."

Fran was shaken, but she went back upstairs and the ladies resumed their meeting. They froze in mid-conversation only a few minutes later when the piano began playing again. Fran crept back downstairs a second time, thinking that there must be an intruder in the building. When she got to the bottom of the stairs, she quickly turned on the lights and the music stopped. She was alone in the room.

"Not only was I alone, but there was simply no way the piano could have played. The cover had never even been removed. It was still on the piano."

We had been standing beside the piano as she told her story. There had been no music during the service and the piano was completely hidden beneath a heavy quilted cover. It would be impossible to strike a single note from it with the cover in place.

"What do you think happened?" Mary asked.

Fran could not offer any explanations for what she and the Ladies of the Castle had heard, but said that other unexplainable sounds, such as the tinkling of silverware and glasses, and disembodied voices, were sometimes heard in the building.

Fran offered one more story about yet another female ghost. During a New Year's Eve party at the castle, a woman dressed in red was seen descending the stairs from the second floor to the first. The partygoers saw the woman move across the room toward the door, which opened of its own accord as she drew near. She passed through the door and out across new-fallen snow. She disappeared in the night and left no footprints.

The Reverend Leonetta Bugleisi is no longer the minister at the

Beverly Unitarian Church, having moved to new pastoral duties in Michigan, but she had several ghost stories of her own while she was there.

Leonetta was talking with some friends and her husband at a church reception in 1994. "I saw two thin woman's arms wrap around my husband's waist," she told me, "and I thought someone was hugging him to say goodnight for the evening. When I looked around him I did not see a face. I said, 'Michael, are you okay?' And he said, 'Yes, why?' I asked him if he felt anything around his waist and he said no. Then the arms disappeared."

Leonetta said that a former custodian had heard the piano playing when no one else was in the building. Another custodian suddenly died in the nursery school hallway while waxing the floors. The summer after his death Leonetta was alone in the upstairs library, sorting through some books. She came across a book about death and dying by Elizabeth Kubler-Ross and put it aside before going downstairs. When she came back up to get the book, it had disappeared and she never found it again. "My theory," Leonetta said, "is that Kevin, the custodian, was still inhabiting the castle he loved so much and took the book as a sign of his existence."

Another time, Leonetta was upstairs with a church member. While Leonetta was in a storage room the other woman was in the apartment area. The woman went down to the first floor unbeknownst to Leonetta, who called out to her.

"When I looked out towards the apartment door I saw a distinct black shadow—and this was in broad daylight—flow down the stairs past me and go to the second floor," Leonetta said.

The fellowship of the Beverly Unitarian Church may never learn the identity of the ghosts who haunt its church, but it doesn't really matter. Those ghosts will always be accepted there and offered haven.

Biograph Theater

CHICAGO

JOHN DILLINGER LIVES. NOT THE FLESH-AND-BLOOD gangster, of course, but his ghost, who has been seen outside the place where Dillinger drew his last breath—the Biograph Theater on North Lincoln Avenue.

By the time Dillinger was gunned down by FBI agents on July 22, 1934, he had become Public Enemy No. 1, his notorious exploits ballyhooed in newspapers across the country on an almost daily basis. While much of the American public viewed Dillinger as something of a modern-day Robin Hood, FBI director J. Edgar Hoover had issued a "shoot to kill" order on the gangster as well as a $10,000 reward. Each of the five states in which Dillinger and his gang had robbed banks also offered $10,000 rewards.

Born in Indianapolis in 1903, John Dillinger was not known as a troublesome youth. Rather, he was quiet, a good student, and a talented baseball player. But in 1923 he was refused permission to marry his sweetheart by the girl's stepfather and, in a rage, he stole a car, abandoning it only a few hours later. Afraid that he might be arrested for the theft, Dillinger enlisted in the U.S. Navy. The Navy wasn't to his liking, however, and he went AWOL several times, finally jumping ship for good in Boston. Listed as a deserter by the Navy, Dillinger made his way back home to Indiana. It wasn't long before he fell in with men who would set him on a life of crime.

In 1924 Dillinger was involved in a robbery in which the victim was accidentally shot. He was convicted and sent to the Indiana State Reformatory. Just as he did in the Navy, Dillinger tried to escape several times, but was always caught. Dillinger became good friends with bank robbers Harry Pierpont and Homer Van Meter, both of whom were shortly after transferred to the state prison in Michigan City. Dillinger himself was later transferred to Michigan City, where he renewed his friendship with the two men. They also introduced him to other inmates who served as worthy professors in his criminal education. A plan was hatched in which Dillinger, who was slated for release before the other men, would rob banks in order to raise money to finance a prison break of the others. Dillinger's notorious bank robbing career was launched.

In July 1933, Dillinger and Harry Copeland walked into the Commercial Bank in Danville, Indiana, pointed guns at the tellers and customers and politely announced that they were robbing the bank. Dillinger, wearing a straw boater, which would become his trademark, was cool and collected. The men made off with $3,500. From that point on Dillinger engaged in a string of bank robberies throughout the Midwest, raising money to break his friends out of prison. When he had enough money, he bought guns and had them smuggled into the Michigan City prison.

While Dillinger's friends in prison were planning their break, he was arrested in Dayton, Ohio, where he had been visiting a girlfriend. He was incarcerated in the Lima, Ohio, jail when ten inmates of the Michigan City prison, using the guns Dillinger had sent them, drove right through the prison's front gates in cars stolen from inside the prison. Some of them discovered Dillinger's whereabouts, broke into the jail, shot the sheriff dead, and freed their friend.

Dillinger and his friends shifted their operations to Chicago, living in a few apartments on the North Side. At one point they raided a police arsenal in Peru, Indiana, and made off with an assortment of weapons, including machine guns, shotguns, and bulletproof vests. Dillinger and his friends robbed banks in Greencastle, Indiana, and Milwaukee before taking a break in Florida and then Arizona. But the law caught up with Dillinger in Tucson. He was arrested and sent back to Illinois to stand trail for the robbery of a bank in East Chicago. Ironically, it was a robbery that, in all likelihood, he did not commit, although he was accused of it.

He was locked up in the "escape-proof" Crown Point, Indiana, prison from which he escaped a month later using a "gun" carved out of a bar of soap and colored black with shoe polish. Taking a few guards hostage, he stole a car from the prison and drove across the state line to Illinois, where he released the guards with his apologies and handed them four dollars for food and carfare. Although he was free again, Dillinger's transportation of kidnapped persons across state lines was a federal offense and now allowed the FBI to become involved in trying to bring him to justice.

Dillinger moved to St. Paul, Minnesota, where he teamed up with old friend and new parolee Homer Van Meter and an angry, deranged killer named Lester Gillis, better known as "Baby Face Nelson." They knocked over a bank in Sioux Falls, South Dakota, but encountered resistance, making off with only about $50,000 of the $200,000 the bank had in the vault. Dillinger and John Hamilton, another old robber friend who had rejoined Dillinger, were shot in the holdup, although their wounds were not severe and they both recovered.

All this time, the FBI was hot on Dillinger's trail. Dillinger, Van Meter, and a woman named Billie Frechette narrowly avoided capture at the St. Paul apartment they were renting. The three escaped in a hail of gunfire, one slug tearing into Dillinger's leg. The trio escaped to an isolated fishing camp in the woods of Wisconsin called Little

Bohemia. There Baby Face Nelson, Eddie Green, John Hamilton, Tommy Carroll, and several of the gang's girlfriends joined them.

Melvin Purvis, director of the Chicago office of the FBI, received a tip that the Dillinger gang was holed up at Little Bohemia. He assembled a team of dozens of agents and planned an attack on the fishing lodge. He positioned his men for a raid on the lodge the night of April 22, 1934. That night the agents saw three men exit a cabin and get into a car. The agents called for them to stop, but the men apparently did not hear the order. The agents opened fire, blasting the car apart and killing Civilian Conservation Corps worker Eugene Boiseneau and wounding two fishermen.

The real crooks heard the gunfire and disappeared into the dark woods. The agents poured gunfire into the cabins all night long, but in the morning all they found were some of the gang members' girlfriends, who had managed to find refuge from the fire by hiding in the basement. Not one of the bank robbers was captured. Hoover and Purvis were embarrassed and incensed by the disaster. They vowed that such a fiasco would never happen again.

In July 1934, Chicago police detective Martin Zarkovich approached Purvis and told him that he could deliver Dillinger. Zarkovich had a friend named Anna Sage, a whorehouse madam who was facing deportation to her native Romania, who he said could set up Dillinger if the FBI would halt her deportation proceedings. The deal was struck.

The evening of July 22 was a warm one. John Dillinger wore a lightweight coat with a white shirt, gray pants, canvas shoes, and his usual straw boater as he entered the Biograph Theater with his most recent girlfriend, Polly Hamilton Keele. Anna Sage, who wore a brilliant orange dress, accompanied the couple. The banner hanging below the Biograph's illuminated marquee advertised that the theater was "cooled by refrigeration" so that its patrons could watch *Manhattan Melodrama*, starring Clark Gable, William Powell, and Myrna Loy, in comfort.

While the movie played, Purvis positioned his men in the streets outside the theater. He was nervous, chain-smoking cigarettes as he waited for the theatergoers to exit. At about 10:30, the house lights came up and the theater began to empty. As the crowd filed out, Purvis saw Anna Sage's distinctive orange dress—the means by which they agreed to identify her, and thus, Dillinger—among the crowd. He signaled to his agents and the police to move in.

Dillinger stepped off the curb, just before the alley that ran alongside the theater. Alerted by something, he suddenly stopped and whirled around, apparently reaching for a gun hidden beneath his coat. The agents opened fire. Three bullets struck him. Dillinger staggered a few steps then fell to the pavement dead.

On the day I visited it, the Biograph Theater looked pretty much as it had that night in 1934. The same imposing marquee still projected out above the sidewalk as it had when Dillinger walked beneath it. The little box office where he had purchased his tickets was still there. But the interior of the Biograph would have been unrecognizable to Dillinger's ghost. At one time a single large room, it had since been dived into smaller theaters. The original seats, including the one that Dillinger had sat in and which had been painted a color different from all the others after his death, were long gone, replaced with newer ones. There were no moviegoers when I was there, but I did speak with the theater manager, as well as some employees, none of whom had ever experienced any ghostly happenings at the theater.

Still, there are stories of people seeing a shadowy figure of a man running on the sidewalk, or heading for the alley. He runs, then staggers, then falls and disappears, almost as if reenacting the shooting over and over again. There are some who say the man killed at the Biograph Theater that night was not really John Dillinger, but that the FBI, embarrassed by the Little Bohemia debacle, could not admit yet another mistake and so covered up the truth. We may never know the truth, but what we do know is that a man was shot and killed that night and that his ghost relives that agony still.

Ghosts of the *Eastland*

CHICAGO

The steamer *Eastland* lying on its side in the Chicago River shortly after capsizing.

ONE OF THE MOST TRAGIC MARITIME DISASTERS in U.S. history did not occur on the storm-tossed seas of the Atlantic or Pacific Oceans, nor was it the result of monstrous icebergs, killer storms, or enemy torpedoes. No, there was nothing dramatic in the death of the steamer *Eastland* except that it slowly rolled onto its side on the Chicago River, in the heart of that city, in plain view of thousands of people, killing at least 844 passengers and wiping out twenty-two entire families. The disaster occurred in water no more than twenty feet deep and only a few feet away from dry land.

Today, these unfortunate victims haunt the stretch of the Chicago River between the Clark and La Salle Street bridges. Witnesses have seen faces peering up at them from the watery depths of the river and have heard unexplainable screams and cries emanating from it. And it could be that the ghosts of the *Eastland* roam even farther into the city.

Saturday, July 24, 1915, dawned as a partly cloudy day in Chicago but the clouds could not dampen the carnival atmosphere among the seven thousand employees of the Western Electric Company who crowded the docks along the south bank of the river near the Clark Street Bridge. The adults chatted and laughed, while their children chased each other as they all awaited their turn to board one of several steamers chartered by Western Electric to take them to the company's annual picnic in Michigan City.

The *Eastland* was one of the newer ships gathered at the docks that day and would be one of the first to depart, so it was natural that many of the picnickers would try to get on board. Rumors had circulated among the steamship lines that the *Eastland* was top-heavy and less than stable, but those rumors were disregarded as passengers began to stream aboard at 6:40 a.m. Only one minute later, the ship began to list starboard, toward the docks. The listing did not overly concern the ship's chief engineer, Joseph Erickson, since it was an expected result of the passengers boarding from that side of the ship. Still, he ordered the ballast tanks on the port side to be filled in order to level the ship. As more passengers crowded on board, the ship began to list to the port side, where many people had congregated to watch the other ships boarding and to listen to a band aboard the nearby *Theodore Roosevelt* play "I'm on My Way to Dear Old Dublin Bay." The *Eastland* crew continued to manipulate the ballast tanks to stabilize the vessel, but still there was no sense of impending danger.

The ship continued to sway back and forth, some of the passengers joking about it as loose objects slid along the deck. Water began entering the *Eastland* on the lower port side. The gangplank had been removed on the overcrowded ship, which now held more than twenty-five hundred passengers. More passengers moved to the port side, increasing the list to forty-five degrees. The crew began to worry and started to move some of the passengers to the starboard side. Water continued to enter the ship from below. Chairs, picnic baskets, and other items fell over and slid across the deck. Passengers below deck began climbing out of gangways and windows on the starboard side as the ship continued to lean toward port. The passengers panicked. They tried to find purchase somewhere on the tilting deck, while those below scrambled to make it topside before the ship keeled over. The ship continued to list dangerously to port. Before the eyes of hundreds of horrified spectators on nearby streets and docks, the *Eastland* slowly rolled over onto its port side.

The body of a woman being recovered from the *Eastland*.

Many passengers were pitched into the Chicago River, where, encumbered by suits and long dresses they were pulled below the water. Many more were trapped below, where they drowned. The thick smoke that filled the ship when some of its machinery exploded killed some. Lucky survivors managed to climb onto the hull of the ship while others were pulled from the river by rescuers in boats and even by onlookers who jumped into the river to save the floundering passengers. Others struggled to stay afloat and clung to whatever floating debris they could find.

Police and firemen and other rescuers climbed onto the hull of the *Eastland*, where they cut holes in the metal plate to bring up the survivors and the dead. Screams echoed all around them from the river and those trapped below deck. They worked frantically to free those inside but the screams gradually diminished even as they worked. By 8 a.m. all the survivors had been rescued, but 844 bodies were pulled from the ship and the river.

The scene was like something from Dante's *Inferno*. One witness, a Chicagoan named Gretchen Krohn, described what it looked like dockside: "Up the slippery wet side canvas was spread that those carrying out the bodies might bring out their gruesome freight at a dog trot and thus empty the overturned basketful of human beings more quickly. All of the bodies carried past were so rigid that poles to carry them seemed superfluous. And the pitiful shortness of most of them! Children, and yet more children. And when it wasn't a child, it was a young girl of eighteen or so."

Another survivor said that the sight of so many babies floating on the water caused him to lose his belief in God.

The Second Regiment Armory on Washington Boulevard was pressed into service as a temporary morgue. The bodies of the victims were transported there to await identification by next of kin. The bodies were laid out in rows of eighty-five. It took several heart-rending days for all of them to be finally identified and claimed.

Today, the original armory building is incorporated into Harpo Studios, which produces the *Oprah Winfrey Show*. It is said that the ghosts of the *Eastland* victims are not at peace in the building. According to Chicago ghosthunter Dale Kaczmarek, one common apparition is the Lady in Gray, the shadowy figure of a woman in a long, flowing dress and ornate hat who is seen drifting through the halls. Supposedly, her image has even been captured on the building's security monitors. In addition to the Lady in Gray, studio employees and security guards have reported hearing crying, the laughter of children, and old-time music. The footsteps of crowds of invisible people are heard going up and down the lobby staircase, accompanied by opening and slamming doors.

Another location that ghosts of the *Eastland* are rumored to haunt is Excalibur, a nightclub housed in the Romanesque-style brick building originally constructed for the Chicago Historical Society in

Excalibur nightclub

1892. Some people think that *Eastland* victims were also brought to the Historical Society, as well as the armory, although Dale Kaczmarek could find no evidence of that taking place. Still, something strange is going on at Excalibur. The events were first noticed in 1985, when a previous nightclub, Limelight, opened in the building. Glasses would fall over and break without anyone being near them and other objects would fall over as well. The balls on the pool table would roll around apparently of their own volition, as if some unseen pool players were enjoying a game.

In 1997, a segment of the television show *Sightings* was filmed at Excalibur featuring host Tim White, a local ghosthunter, and a psychic. The psychic heard a child's voice say, "Stop and watch me." Excalibur employees have heard small voices, like children, crying and have seen a little girl looking over the railing in the club's Dome Room. Adult figures have been seen in the club as well, including a white-tuxedoed figure and a bluish-colored shape that floated up the stairs. We will probably never know if these ghosts are connected to the *Eastland* disaster, but whether they are or not, they add more interest to an already fascinating and macabre story.

Glessner House
CHICAGO

THE FIRST THING KERRY*, THE YOUNG DOCENT
at Glessner House told me as we stood in the courtyard behind the
building, was that I could not use his real name in my story. According
to the folks at the Prairie Avenue House Museums, the nonprofit
organization that operates and maintains Glessner House and two
other historic homes in the Prairie Avenue Historic District—and
the same folks who sign Kerry's paycheck—the 1887 mansion is
absolutely not haunted.

That's not what Kerry says.

While my wife, Mary, rested on a bench before Glessner House,
waiting for the official tour to begin, I walked through the mansion's
porte-cochere and wandered around to the courtyard. Glessner House

sits at the corner of Prairie Avenue and Eighteenth Street. Its exterior is made of rugged, rough-hewn stone with Romanesque elements and the steeply pitched gable roof is made of red tile. The mansion looks like a fortress and, indeed, that is what the Glessner family's snobby neighbors called it after the house had been completed.

The rear of the mansion, however, sports a much different style. The famed architect Henry Hobson Richardson designed the house and it was his intent to design the courtyard and rear of the house as a comfortable refuge from the busy street. Here, the walls are faced with pinkish brick trimmed at the lintels and sills with cream-colored limestone. Unlike the severe planes of the mansion's street-side façade, three turrets projecting into the courtyard punctuate the rear of the building. All the rooms inside the four-story mansion are oriented toward the landscaped courtyard and large windows open out to it.

It was a beautiful sunny day, and I was the only person admiring the courtyard until Kerry showed up. He was congenial and well versed on the history of the house and the Glessner family and wasted no time in relating it to me.

"Any ghosts?" I asked, experience having taught me it was best to get to the point in paranormal matters.

Kerry gave me a sidelong glance and took a step away, as if I had given him a shove. "No ghosts," he said, shaking his head.

I still had a few minutes before the house tour was scheduled to commence, so I continued to stroll through the courtyard. Kerry stuck by me, pointing out interesting architectural details. We stopped at the rear of the courtyard. I was looking up at the servants' quarters above the kitchen in the west wing of the house.

"But some weird things have happened here," Kerry said, almost in a whisper.

Bingo.

"Really? Like what?"

Kerry looked around to make sure we were still alone. "Both Glessners died in the house. Mrs. Glessner in 1932 and her husband in 1936."

"That's not weird," I said, "just unfortunate."

"But they're still here," Kerry said, "at least Mr. Glessner."

We started slowly walking out to the front of the mansion. Kerry told me about the day he was in the mansion's kitchen, located at one end of the west wing. He said that he suddenly detected the scent of Mr. Glessner's favorite soap, a sample of which is on display in his dressing room. Glessner's dressing room, located off the master bedroom, is at the opposite end of the mansion, a great distance from the kitchen. Unless Glessner's favorite soap was Eau d'Skunk, it was unlikely its fragrance could be detected that far away under normal circumstances.

"It was intense," Kerry said. "It was like someone held the soap right up under my nose."

As strange as Kerry's story sounded, olfactory sensations are frequently linked to ghostly manifestations. It is not unusual for people to detect a female ghost through the fragrances of a favorite perfume or flower. Male ghosts, at least those who smoked in life, may be recognized by the scent of a favorite cigar or pipe tobacco. I had never heard of soap fragrance as an indicator of a ghostly presence, but I supposed it was as plausible as the other scents.

Besides, John Jacob Glessner was the kind of man who would continue to make his presence known long after death. Glessner was born in Zanesville, Ohio, in 1834. As a young man he was employed by Warder, Bushnell and Glessner, manufacturers of farm machinery. The ambitious Glessner worked his way up through the corporate ranks and in 1870 was sent to Chicago to oversee the company's operations there. That same year, Glessner married Frances Macbeth of Springfield, Ohio.

The Glessners occupied two different houses before constructing the Prairie Avenue mansion. Their son George was born in one in 1871 and their daughter Frances, called Fanny, was born in the second house in 1875.

It was in the fashionable lakeshore Prairie Avenue District that Glessner built his mansion, a home much different in style from those of his rich neighbors. This was a neighborhood of tree-lined streets and fabulous mansions that displayed the architectural genius of men such as Solon Spencer Beman, Daniel Burnham, Richard Morris Hunt, and John Wellborn Root. The Glessner house was neighbor to other lavish homes owned by men whose names defined commercial success in late-nineteenth-century Chicago. George Pullman, the railroad car magnate, had a fine Victorian home on the corner diagonally across from the Glessner house. The Kimball family, made wealthy by the Kimball organs installed in thousands of churches across America, lived directly across the street from the Glessners. Marshall Field's department stores were located mostly in downtown Chicago, but his house was just down the street from the Glessners', as was that of the Armour family, the famous meatpackers.

The lifestyle in these opulent mansions, filled with fine furniture, antiques, and art treasures from all around the world, was grand and it took an army of people to keep them functioning. There were servants, butlers, doormen, cooks, housecleaners, mechanics, and tutors continually engaged in some task or another. Many of these domestic servants lived in the mansions, receiving food and board as part of their compensation.

Strong competition in Glessner's industry in the early 1900s threatened to destroy some companies, but Glessner was one of the men who successfully helped to merge the corporation with some of the leading firms of the day, including McCormick Reaper and Deering. The new corporation took the name International Harvester and was an instant financial success. John Glessner was rewarded for his services by being named a vice-president in the new organization; he went from being a merely wealthy man to a fabulously wealthy one.

The Glessners were prominent members of Chicago society. John Glessner served as trustee of the Art Institute of Chicago and the Chicago Orchestral Association, was director of the Chicago Relief and Aid Society, and was president of the board of Rush Medical College. Frances Glessner, John's wife, was a member of the Chicago Society of Decorative Art and founded the Monday Morning Reading Class for women; the group met weekly in the Glessner house for more than thirty years.

The Glessners loved their Prairie Avenue home and lived there for fifty years, even as many of the other grand old houses surrounding them were closing up because of the enormous costs in operating them. The neighborhood was changing and, one by one, the wonderful old mansions were either being pulled down or were subdivided into boarding houses.

Today, only five of these elegant Prairie Avenue homes remain, although the neighborhood is enjoying a revitalization of sorts as affluent Chicagoans are rediscovering it. The Glessner House is the best preserved of the old houses. Mary and I were about to see how well preserved the old mansion was; the house tour was about to start.

We joined the dozen or so people milling about on the sidewalk before the massive wooden front door of the house. Kerry stood off to the side since he was not leading this group. Our tour guide soon joined us. She was a thin, grim-faced woman with a sharp profile who set off around the house on a double-time quickstep that soon left the elderly and portly among the group panting somewhere far behind us. She was every bit as well informed about the house as Kerry, and I supposed she liked her job, but she never smiled so I was not at all certain.

We entered the house, the first stop being the basement, which was like no basement I had ever been in before. No leaking water heater. No smelly, smoky furnace. No insulation drooping down from exposed rafters overhead. No, the Glessner basement, at least the portion we saw on the tour, was carpeted, paneled in maple and furnished with beautiful bookcases, tables and chairs. Yellow pine beams supported the ceiling. This room was the schoolroom, built for George Glessner, who suffered severe allergies and was schooled at home. Architect Henry Richardson designed an effective cross-ventilation system especially for the schoolroom to help alleviate young George's sufferings.

The upper levels of the mansion were designed in imitation of an English country manor. Red-oak paneling lined the halls, the parlor, the library, and dining room, and was also used in the wainscoting in the spiral staircase and upstairs passages. Huge oak beams held up the ceiling in the main entry hall, library, and dining room. So much wood would have made any house dark as a medieval castle, but Richardson solved this problem by having all the rooms face out to the courtyard in the rear and including large windows on that side of the house to let in ample light.

Much of the furniture and decorations in the house were not actually owned by the Glessners, but were authentic to the time and similar to the possessions the Glessners might have owned. The library, however, was an exception in that almost all of the books and furnishings in the room were original to the Glessners.

The tour guide led us into the library, trying to squeeze us all into the narrow aisle defined by the velvet cord separating us from the interior of the room. We had rapidly outpaced the stragglers. As she began to tell us about the library, more of them arrived, plowing into the group, rapidly squeezing the oxygen out of the room. I saw Mary disappear in a corner and thought I would probably never see her again.

From what I could see over the shoulders of those in front of me, bookcases lined the room, filled with leather-bound books on a wide variety of topics. Framed prints and paintings lined the walls above the bookcases and valuable ceramic pieces stood on the top shelves. One of the ten fireplaces in the house was located in the library, this one faced with glazed tile.

A huge desk stood in the center of the room, covered with pieces of art, framed photos, and the usual desk clutter. A rare life mask of Abraham Lincoln, along with casts of his hands, rested upon the desk. It looked as though he were trapped inside the desk and struggling to climb out.

Somehow, we all filed out of the library—Mary had survived the crush after all—and followed our guide to the Glessner's master bedroom. In one little alcove was John Glessner's dressing room. A black suit coat of 1920s style hung from the back of a chair. A beaver top hat rested upon the seat. Upon a narrow shelf on one wall was arranged some of Glessner's toiletries, including a bottle of bay rum and three bars of soap. This was the same soap that Kerry had smelled in the kitchen, although I could not detect its scent only a few feet away.

As the group left the master bedroom, I saw Kerry following

behind us. I dropped back to talk with him.

We spoke in low tones, both of us fearful of being shushed by our school-marm tour guide.

"I didn't smell it," I said.

"No?" said Kerry.

I shook my head. "Of course, I have hay fever right now and can't smell much of anything, so maybe what I think doesn't matter."

"There's other stuff, too," Kerry said, casting a glance at the tour guide up front. She was deep into her lecture and paid us no mind.

"I've heard my name called," Kerry said. "There was no one else around and I heard it very distinctly, clear as a bell. 'Kerry.' Not once, but twice."

"You're sure there was no one else with you?"

"Positive," Kerry said, "and, I know this sounds strange, but somehow I was sure the voice was that of John Glessner."

Strange? Not at all.

We had followed the group to the kitchen at the rear of the west wing, the very room in which Kerry had smelled the aroma of Glessner's soap.

"And I'm not the only one who has felt things here," Kerry said.

He told me about a maintenance man who was working alone in the shop when he suddenly felt a strong hand grasp his shoulder. The invisible hand squeezed the man's shoulder but, according to Kerry, the man said the squeeze was not painful or frightening, but was more encouraging.

"The guy said that it was as though Glessner were there supervising his work and giving him a gentle squeeze to show that he was pleased," Kerry said.

John Glessner lived in the house he loved for fifty years and eventually died there. Maybe he has found it difficult to move on and leave the place he treasured all those years, or perhaps he just wants to hang around to see what happen to his old neighborhood. In any case, he remains, master of the house.

Graceland Cemetery

CHICAGO

GRACELAND CEMETERY ON NORTH CLARK STREET was one of those beautiful parklike cemeteries that were in vogue in the late nineteenth century. Beautiful, sometimes ornate funerary art marked the graves of some of Chicago's leading citizens where they slept among well-trimmed lawns and old shade trees. Meatpacker Phillip Armour, retail legend Marshall Field, hotel owner Potter Palmer, private detective Allan Pinkerton, and railroad car tycoon George Pullman were all buried there, as was William A. Hulbert, the

National League of Professional Baseball Clubs' second president, from 1877–1882, who rested beneath a huge granite baseball adorned with the league's team names.

It was a late summer's afternoon when my wife, Mary, and I visited Graceland. The trees cast long, cool shadows across the emerald lawns. We appeared to be alone. Other than the occasional birdcall, it was quiet and peaceful in the cemetery. I could understand why it was once fashionable for people to picnic there, or to simply enjoy the beauty and tranquility of the place. Having grown up in New England, I was used to ancient cemeteries filled with worn, moss-covered stones, most of them broken or leaning in all directions like bad teeth. You just knew those cemeteries were filled with ghosts. By comparison, no one could have thought that such a lovely place as Graceland was haunted. But it was.

One of the hauntings concerned the tomb of a man named Ludwig Wolff. It may very well have been only a legend, based on the man's last name, but it was said that his tomb was guarded by a ghostly dog with glowing green eyes that howled mournfully at the moon. As it was a bright, sunny day, I did not see the ghost dog, but as I passed by the tomb, I did wonder why a ghost dog would appear there. Was the dog Wolff's pet? Was it, in fact, a wolf? And if Wolff himself haunted the cemetery, would that make him a wolfman instead of a ghost? Those were the questions that entered this ghosthunter's mind.

The whole concept of cemeteries being good places to find ghosts has been under discussion recently. Many psychic researchers believe that ghosts haunt places that have some meaningful relevance to their former lives. Sometimes these places recalled happy times in their lives; the houses in which they were children or perhaps, the houses in which they raised their own families. On a grimmer note, these places could be prisons or hospitals, or other places in which they spent unhappy, traumatic, or eventful times. But why a cemetery, a place where no living person longs to be and a place that, at most, is only a brief stopping point between death and the hereafter? If you were a ghost, would you rather wander around some old cemetery, or would you rather go back to your home or to some other happy place? Still, ghosts are found in cemeteries, possibly because they are somehow trapped there, bound to the spot in a psychic force that we do not understand. Noted psychic researchers Ed and Lorraine Warren would say that cemeteries are spawning grounds for evil spirits and may be portals to a nasty and demonic realm. My own experiences have shown me that far more hauntings occur out of cemeteries than in them.

Statue of Inez Clarke

Graceland, however, did have its ghosts.

The most noted Graceland ghost was that of little Inez Clarke, who died in 1880 at the age of six, apparently killed by lightning while on a family picnic. Her grief-stricken parents commissioned a life-sized statue of their daughter to be placed upon a stone base above her grave. The statue was shielded from the elements by a protective glass box.

I was completely charmed by the details of the little girl's statue. Inez sat in a rough-hewn chair wearing a pretty frilled dress. The ribbons of her hat were loosely fastened around her neck, although the hat itself was slung over one shoulder. She wore a locket on a chain and held a parasol in her right hand. But what held me most was her face. Her eyes seemed simultaneously fastened on mine and fixed on some greater distance, an eternal point to which I was not privy. Looking into her eyes, I felt as though some communion were possible there. But the most evocative feature of her face was her enigmatic smile, a barely discernible Mona Lisa-like upturn to the lips, that seemed to say Inez had a secret.

The stories associated with the ghost of Inez included strange weeping sounds that were heard near the statue, as well as the vision of a child who would vanish into thin air near her grave. The most interesting stories, however, concerned the statue itself. It is said that sometimes the statue would disappear from within its glass box. This had been noted especially during thunderstorms, which seemed to make sense since the child was killed by lightning. Perhaps poor Inez belatedly ran for cover as she relived the awful day she died. In *Haunted Illinois* psychic researcher Troy Taylor says that more than one security guard at Graceland had seen the empty box, only to later find the statue had returned to its usual place inside. A guard quit shortly after finding the glass box empty one night.

There was no one around the day I visited, so I was not able to get any firsthand accounts about Inez's wandering spirit. If she was out there, however, I hoped she was enjoying a paranormal picnic at Graceland, without the lightning.

Another story from Graceland was not so much a ghost story as it was simply a weird legend. The final resting place of Dexter Graves—I'm serious, that's his name—was marked by a larger-than-life statue called "Eternal Silence." It was an extremely creepy statue of a brooding man wrapped up in a voluminous robe. One arm, buried beneath the folds of the robe, was raised parallel to the ground, covering the mouth and lower half of the face. Only the eyes and nose were visible beneath the cowl of the robe. Over the years since Graves died in 1831, the effects of weather had turned the statue pale green, all except for the face, which remained black, having been protected from the weather by the robe's deep folds.

The legend says that anyone looking into the figure's face will catch a glimpse of his own death. That legend did not come true for me, nor did the one that says the statue simply cannot be photographed. There was also some vague doom associated with rubbing the figure's nose, but it was too tall for me to reach it, so I was spared. At least for now. You just have to wonder how such dumb and easily discredited legends get started. Haunted or not, an awesome power and majesty emanated from "Eternal Silence." In the absence of any obvious ghosts, it made the trip to Graceland worthwhile.

Jane Addams Hull-House Museum
CHICAGO

SOCIAL REFORMERS JANE ADDAMS AND ELLEN GATES Starr founded Hull-House on Chicago's Near West Side, a once-fashionable area that had become by 1889, a run-down industrial neighborhood, rife with poverty, crime, sickness, and illiteracy. It was a neighborhood full of smoky factories, squalid sweatshops, saloons, and crumbling tenement houses inhabited mostly by poor immigrant Germans, Greeks, Italians, and Polish and Russian Jews. There was no better neighborhood for these pioneering women to test the purpose of the Hull-House charter, as Addams herself defined it in her book, *Twenty Years at Hull-House*: "To provide a center for higher civic and social life; to institute and maintain educational and philanthropic enterprises, and to investigate and improve conditions in the industrial districts of Chicago."

The original building in the Hull-House Settlement, which eventually grew to a dozen sprawling buildings by the time the facility closed in 1963, was the Charles Hull house built in 1856, in what was then one of the affluent suburban areas of Chicago. By the time Addams and Starr came across the house in 1889, the bucolic suburbs had been swallowed up by the rapidly growing city of Chicago. Sandwiched between a saloon and undertaker's establishment, the ground floor of this faded beauty of a home was rented as office and storage space for the factory behind it, but the women were able to rent the second floor and one room on the first floor to begin their venture.

It is in this house that the ghost stories originate.

Charles Hull was a Chicago real estate promoter whose wife died in the house he had built at 800 South Halsted Street shortly after the family moved in, leaving him a widower with two small children. His wife's cousin, Helen Culver, moved in to take care of the children, although she left them during the Civil War to serve as a nurse. Sometime after her return, the children became ill and, despite her nursing abilities, died. In 1868, Hull closed up the house and moved out.

Even though it was abandoned, the house somehow survived the Great Chicago Fire of 1871. Culver inherited the house when Hull died, and she rented it out to several tenants, including the Little Sisters of the Poor, who ran a home for the elderly; a used furniture store; and the factory that occupied it when Jane Addams first saw it.

All that time, the house was haunted.

Addams mentioned the fact that the house was haunted in *Twenty Years at Hull-House*. She wrote: "It had a half-skeptical reputation for a haunted attic, so far respected by the tenants living on the second floor that they always kept a large pitcher full of water on the attic stairs. Their explanation of this custom was so incoherent that I was sure it was a survival of the belief that a ghost could not cross running water, but perhaps that interpretation was only my eagerness for finding folklore."

A bucket of water is not running water and the resident spirit, believed to be that of Mrs. Hull, apparently had no qualms about wandering around the house. Later stories tell of strange footsteps in the night, especially in a second-floor bedroom occupied by Addams, which was the same bedroom of the dead mistress of the house. After enduring several nights of loud footsteps in her otherwise empty bedroom, Addams finally gave the room back to the ghost of Mrs. Hull and moved to another room.

Guests of Hull-House also encountered the ghost. Helen Campbell, who was herself a successful author and social reformer with her book, *Prisoners of Poverty*, spent a night in the haunted bedroom. Sleeping fitfully, she awoke and in the dim light saw an unidentifiable figure standing by her bed. She leapt out of bed and turned up the gas jet to illuminate the room, but the apparition had vanished. A dream? Perhaps, but could it not have been Mrs. Hull watching over her guest?

Louise Bowen was a lifelong friend of Addams and she too had the same kind of encounter with the ghost of Hull-House. The same things happened to Jane and Mary Smith, and to Canon Barnett of Toynbee Hall, from the English settlement house upon which Hull-House was modeled. Each of them said they were visited by a lady dressed in white who was able to pass through closed doors.

The docents at the Hull-House Museum, which is now owned by the University of Illinois at Chicago, are forbidden to talk about the ghost. Despite that injunction, Sara*, the young graduate student who guided my wife, Mary, and me through Hull-House, confided that many people who worked there had experienced strange things— sounds for which they could find no source, motion detectors that went off without anyone being there, strange shadows, and a sense of uneasiness, as if one should quickly look over his shoulder before whatever it is that is there, disappears. The kind of feeling that truly makes your hair stand on end.

Another strange story that attached itself to Hull-House was the tale of the Devil Baby. Sometime in 1913, a rumor spread through the neighborhood that a devil baby, complete with horns and a tail, had been born at Hull-House, and that it was being kept alive in the locked attic of the house by Addams and her staff. No one knows how the rumor began, but it persisted for several years and Addams herself, baffled by the rumor, spent much energy in debunking it. Over a period of time, it died out, although the story provided the inspiration for Ira Levin's 1967 best-selling novel, *Rosemary's Baby.*

It was a warm and sunny August day when Mary and I visited Hull-House, not at all the kind of day one would consider even remotely creepy. We were the only visitors at that time, despite the fact that beyond the windows, outside, we could see streams of students hauling mattresses, TVs, clothes, and computers from their cars to the dorms as they moved in to begin the new school year.

Sara told us that we were welcome to tour the ground-floor rooms of Hull-House but that the second floor, the floor on which Mrs. Hull's bedroom was located, was off-limits to visitors. An elegant wood-carved staircase in the foyer, carpeted with a red rug, led to the second floor. I was tempted to go up anyway, but decided to obey the rules. Since I didn't see any buckets of water on the stairs, I thought maybe the ghost would come down to visit with us.

Sara said that she would show us a brief video about the history of Hull-House, and we followed her out the back door to the adjoining residents' Dining Hall, which was reconstructed in 1967, as was the main house. The Dining Hall and Hull-House itself are the only two buildings left of the many buildings that made up the Settlement. Just as she approached the door to the Dining Hall, Sara stopped abruptly.

"Oh, dear," she said, looking down at the sidewalk. There lay a dead bird, its barred wings spread wide as if in flight.

A good omen, I thought.

Sara paused for a moment, then stepped around the little corpse and unlocked the door to the Dining Hall. "I'll call someone from maintenance to pick it up," she said.

She led us upstairs to a large, rather nondescript room, in which was set up a screen and rows of chairs. She ran the video for us, an interesting story about how Hull-House came to be, but I was disappointed that there was no mention of its ghost. When the video was over, Sara brought us downstairs to view the residents' Dining Hall.

The residents of Hull-House were not the poor immigrants from the neighborhood. Rather, they were young, idealistic men and women, mostly college educated, who came to live and work at Hull-House and direct its programs. They did this as volunteers, without pay. Many of these residents were women who in all likelihood would not have found a suitable outlet for the application of their college education had they not worked at Hull-House. In the Dining Hall, these bright and energetic young people had the opportunity to socialize with each other and to exchange ideas and opinions in ways that they might not have had in the general public.

The Dining Hall, with its wood paneling, paintings, carpeted floors, and long tables, seemed like a comfortable enough place to dine and chat, but now it was quiet and still, devoid of any ghostly presence.

I glanced at Mary and she shook her head. She didn't feel anything either.

We left the Dining Hall and went back out to Hull-House. The dead bird was gone.

Back inside Hull-House, we were free to explore the downstairs rooms at our leisure. Jane Addams had wanted to restore the fine old house as best she could, to make it a warm and welcoming place for the poor people of the neighborhood. She succeeded admirably.

Richly carved moldings outlined the tall doors and long windows and framed the ceilings. In the center of the back parlor, Addams's desk, a simple Colonial style in cherry wood with three rail-back chairs, stood on a Persian rug. A bright brass chandelier with six tulip-shaped glass globes hung above the desk. The walls were covered with gold-flocked wallpaper. On one wall was a marble fireplace surround. A portrait of Jane Addams in a gilded frame hung above it. A glass-front bookcase stood against another wall. Sunlight streamed into the quiet and peaceful room through the sheer curtains covering the windows.

If Mrs. Hull was floating around in that room, she didn't make her presence known to either Mary or me.

The smaller room adjoining the back parlor was called the

octagon room, for obvious reasons, and was the "nerve center" of the Settlement. A pigeon hole desk, now only collecting dust, years ago would have been stuffed with messages for Hull-House volunteers. An old-fashioned two-piece phone stood silently on the desk. Nearby, an ancient typewriter slowly rusted away.

These rooms were interesting from a historical perspective, but my imagination was continually drawn to the stairs in the foyer. I stood there before the velvet rope that blocked access to them and looked up. There wasn't much to see, only the light gradually fading into gloom at the top of the stairs.

Although I didn't see anything that day as I peered up into the darkness at the head of the stairs, others have seen strange things. Dale Kaczmarek, a Chicago-area ghosthunter, once took a photo of the stairs, using a standard 35mm camera with infrared film. Although the stairs were empty when he took the photo, four shadowy monk-like figures appeared on the print after the film was developed. This is interesting because there are no known connections between monks and Hull-House, yet monks, or at least dark, hooded figures, are common ghostly apparitions, even in locations in which no monks were ever known to have lived. Other people have reported seeing similar dark and hooded figures in the windows of Hull-House. Who these figures may be, and why they are at Hull-House, remains a mystery.

While the ghostly encounters at Hull-House were originally attributed to Mrs. Hull, some believe that the ghost of Jane Addams herself may also be roaming the rooms in which she spent so much of her life. Perhaps her work there is not yet finished.

Museum of Science and Industry

CHICAGO

CHICAGO'S MUSEUM OF SCIENCE AND INDUSTRY, located at 57th Street and Lake Shore Drive, is one of the country's pre-eminent centers for informal science and technology education.

It is also home to at least three ghosts.

The beautiful domed and columned building was originally built as the Palace of Fine Arts for the 1893 Columbian Exposition and is the only surviving structure from that exposition. The museum, which is situated along the shore of the Jackson Park lagoon, looks more like an ancient Greek temple than it does a center of science and technology.

Perhaps it is that feeling of antiquity that draws the ghosts.

One of the museum's most famous ghosts is that of Clarence Darrow, the celebrated lawyer whose battle with William Jennings Bryan in 1925 over the issue of teaching evolution in schools—a trial known as the Scopes Monkey Trial—has become a landmark case in the annals of jurisprudence and was also the inspiration for the play and movie *Inherit the Wind*. Darrow figured prominently in many other high-profile cases, including the 1924 Leopold and Loeb case, in which he defended two stone-cold teenage murderers of a fourteen-year-old boy and won them life imprisonment instead of the electric chair.

Darrow lived in the Hyde Park neighborhood that includes the museum. He died in Chicago in 1938 and his cremated remains were scattered in the Jackson Park lagoon as he had requested. Every year a wreath-laying ceremony honoring Darrow is held at the bridge spanning the lagoon. In 1957 the bridge was dedicated in his memory and is now known as the Clarence Darrow Memorial Bridge.

Dale Kaczmarek, a Chicago ghost investigator who also operates area ghost tours, reported that a man on one of his tours took photos of the lagoon and captured the smoky image of a face near the bridge. Could it have been the ghost of Clarence Darrow?

"His ghost has been seen here in the museum as well," said Travis*, a docent my wife, Mary, and I met at the Burlington Zephyr exhibit inside the museum. Travis was a rosy-cheeked young man whose new beard was just starting to grow in. Travis wore the blue uniform and cap of a train conductor, but he looked more like a kid on Halloween trick-or-treating as Captain Kangaroo.

"People have seen an elderly man dressed in a suit, walking in the hall by the windows that overlook the lagoon. They say he matches the description of Clarence Darrow. He's there for just a moment, then he disappears," Travis said.

Travis told us how the ghost interrupted a children's Halloween storytelling session he was conducting at the museum. "I looked up and there he was. In the next second he was gone."

We were standing before the gleaming engine of the Burlington

Zephyr, one of the country's first diesel streamlined trains, as we spoke. The stainless steel Burlington Zephyr seemed to glow in the vast, dark hall of the museum. Three cars were attached to the engine: a mail car, a passenger car, and a passenger lounge at the rear of the train that featured a curved exterior and panoramic windows. Travis said he had more to tell us, but it was time for him to lead the next tour through the train. Mary and I climbed aboard with him and a handful of other visitors.

The tour began in the mail car, with the history of the Burlington Zephyr given to us by Zeph, a robotic figure in the form of a talking burro so lifelike that some of the little children in the group patted its nose and tried to feed it some hay while it talked. The real Zeph joined the Dawn to Dusk Club of eighty-four distinguished passengers on the Zephyr's maiden run from Denver to Chicago on May 26, 1934. Zeph came on board when the *Rocky Mountain News* offered the Chicago, Burlington and Quincy Railroad (CB&Q) a "Rocky Mountain Canary" as a mascot for the trip. It was only when the burro was delivered that Ralph Budd, CB&Q president, understood he had accepted a burro and not a bird. Budd quickly ordered hay to be placed on board for Zeph, remarking, "One more jackass on this trip won't make a difference." Zeph sped off into history as the Zephyr broke all train speed records of the day, traveling 1,015 miles in 13 hours and 5 minutes, the longest nonstop train trip the world had ever witnessed. The Zephyr's average speed was 77.5 miles per hour, although it peaked at 112.5 miles per hour.

The Zephyr's sleek styling and incredible speed made it an instant celebrity, and the train starred in the 1934 movie *The Silver Streak*. Streamlining became all the rage in design, copied in everything from cars and airplanes to toasters and vacuum cleaners, and Madison Avenue ad agencies appropriated the Zephyr for advertising campaigns.

At the museum, the next car was the passenger coach. Unlike the stuffy old Pullman coaches, the Zephyr's coach was as streamlined as its gleaming exterior. The clean lines and sleek design were accented by indirect lighting, plush upholstered seats, and colors in soothing pale green, cool blue, and light brown. Passengers could order 20¢ hamburgers and hot dogs, or other food from the kitchen. They were served by the all-female Zephyrettes, on-board hostesses who saw to the passengers' every need. The day we were there, there were no Zephyrettes on board to assist the life-sized plaster passengers, who now sat scattered among the plush seats. Each of the figures had a speaker built into it so that it could "talk" to the others about the train and the journey. It was an eerie feeling, sitting next to these immobile figures, never knowing when the one right beside you might suddenly speak. I noticed that those same little children who so happily had fed the fake Zeph now clung to their parents.

The last car on the tour was the lounge car. Large windows completely lined its sides and rounded back end. A film projected onto the windows gave the illusion of movement while the jostling floor mimicked the rocking of the train along the tracks.

As we stood behind a velvet rope, we watched three robotic figures dressed in the style of the 1930s, seated in comfortable upholstered chairs. Ralph Budd sat on the left wearing a three-piece suit. His sister, Mrs. Katherine Wilder, occupied the center seat. To her left sat her young daughter. They all moved as they chatted with each other, subtle movements such as the turning of a head, a hand moving to one side, the flexing of a foot. There was something secretive and mysterious in these movements, as if the robots were afraid of being caught in the act. I would look at the figure of Budd as it spoke, turning its head to look at me and then detect some movement from one of the other figures. Weren't Mrs. Wilder's hands folded in her lap before? Wasn't the daughter looking to her left only a few second ago? The figures were more than lifelike, they were just plain creepy.

The tour ended in the lounge car and we all debarked from there. Travis had a break for a few minutes so we resumed our conversation while Mary wandered off to explore more of the museum.

"That was a great tour," I said.

"Thanks." Travis took off his conductor's hat, wiped the sweat from his brow with his coat sleeve, and put the hat back on. Apparently, fake conducting on a train that couldn't go anywhere was harder work than

I thought. "What did you think of the animatronics?" Travis asked.

"The which?"

"Animatronics, the robots."

"Really good," I said. "A little freaky maybe."

Travis nodded. "We have to turn them on, you know. They're not able to move unless we do." One of the people who had been on the tour was walking near us and Travis waited for her to pass by before continuing. "So how come the figures in the lounge car move on their own, without being switched on? Mrs. Wilder, especially. She's been seen moving her head when the power's off."

"Do you think the car is haunted?" I asked.

He shrugged and drew me to a display board near the train. One of the panels described an accident at Napier, Missouri, on October 2, 1939, in which the engineer and another person aboard the Burlington Zephyr were killed.

"Maybe there's reason for it to be haunted," Travis said.

We had walked around to the front of the sleek locomotive, its single headlight piercing the gloom of the great hall. Though at rest, it looked as though it could spring to life at any moment and hurtle through the museum, with or without the dead engineer at its controls. More people passed by and Travis lowered his voice when he said, "The train isn't the only thing in the museum that's haunted. Have you heard about the *U-505*?"

I knew something of the history of the *U-505*, the only German submarine ever captured by the Americans in World War II. The *U-505* was commissioned in Hamburg, Germany, in 1941, was involved in several battles, and by 1942 was already responsible for sinking eight allied ships. On June 4, 1944, the U.S.S. *Guadalcanal* task group in the mid-Atlantic Ocean attacked the *U-505*. The Germans attempted to scuttle the sub, were unsuccessful, and so surrendered to the American forces. The capture of the sub was the first time an American naval force had captured an enemy ship on the high seas since 1815, when the U.S.S. *Peacock* seized H.M.S. *Nautilus* during the War of 1812. The submarine was towed into port in Bermuda, where U.S. and British military experts could study it. Its capture was kept a secret until after the war.

In 1946, the U.S. Navy planned to scuttle the German submarine by using her for target practice. The existence of the sub came to the attention of the Museum of Science and Industry's president, Leonard Lohr, who revealed ten-year-old plans for the museum that included a submarine among its future exhibits. The people of Chicago raised $250,000 to purchase the sub and tow it to the museum, where it was designated as a war memorial and became a part of the museum's exhibits.

But none of that was what Travis was talking about. He was talking about ghosts aboard the *U-505*.

"What kind of ghosts?" I asked.

"The commander," Travis said, "a man named Peter Zschech. In 1943, the sub was attacked with depth charges by a British ship. The attack went on for a while and Zschech just lost it. While the depth charges were exploding all around the sub, he killed himself in the control room." Travis told me that the *U-505*'s First Officer took over and skillfully evaded the attacking ship, bringing the sub safely back to port in France. "Some people here think that Zschech is still aboard his sub," Travis said.

He said that before the museum opens, a staff person boards the sub and walks through its length to turn the lights on inside. One day, as a member of the staff walked through the darkened sub to turn on the lights, he suddenly felt an unseen presence with him.

"The guy said that the presence 'tried to enter him,'" said Travis. "Those were his exact words, 'enter him.'"

Another docent was straightening up the commander's bunk, Travis said, when he felt someone right behind him. He whirled around but there was no one there.

Female docents especially seem to be having a tough time with the commander's ghost. One young woman had just made a rather insulting joke about the commander, according to Travis, when a steel door suddenly slammed closed on her hand, injuring her. Another woman felt a hand come out of nowhere and grasp her shoulder. Of course, there was no one else in the room.

The *U-505* exhibit was undergoing major renovations when Mary and I visited the museum. It will be interesting to see if the ghost of Commander Zschech becomes even more active as a result of being stirred up by the commotion, or whether he decides to ship out for some otherworldly port. But even if Zschech leaves, the ghosts of Clarence Darrow and those aboard the Burlington Zephyr remain to keep you company when you visit Chicago's Museum of Science and Industry.

Red Lion Pub

CHICAGO

JOHN CORDWELL WAS A MAN'S MAN IN SO MANY ways. As a Royal Air Force pilot during World War II, he was shot down, captured by the Germans, and became one of the forgers involved in the failed escape from the German prisoner of war camp Stalag Luft III, located near Sagan, Poland; the heroic effort was later immortalized in the 1963 Steve McQueen movie, *The Great Escape*.

After the war, Cordwell moved to Chicago, where he became a renowned architect and city planner. Chicago's popular rapid-transit system probably never would have been built without his guidance and direction. Even while accomplishing all these great things, Cordwell longed for one simple pleasure, to hoist a pint of stout in his own pub, just like the pubs he used to frequent in his native England.

John Cordwell realized his dream in 1984 when he and his son Colin bought a bar at 2446 North Lincoln Avenue on Chicago's North Side, across the street from the infamous Biograph Theater where John Dillinger met his fate, and renamed it the Red Lion Pub. Until his death in 1999, the Red Lion was something of a home away from home for the senior Cordwell.

"But I know my father is still here," said Colin Cordwell, as I sat at the bar with him and his brother-in-law, Nick Rice.

Nick had longish white hair and a receding hairline. He wore a T-shirt that read, A dog is the only relative you get to choose. "We feel him all the time," Nick said.

It was mid-afternoon on a weekday and the pub was not crowded. As I sat at the long bar with the two men, my wife, Mary, sat at a booth by the large window overlooking the street. The sunlight came in through the window, but farther back at the bar, the pub was not as well lit.

"I've got a photo that was recently taken by one of our customers that I'm sure shows my father," Colin said. The photo depicted some people at the bar and a misty figure with a face that Colin recognized as that of his father. "I knew it was my father," Colin said, "because he had his hand on the girl's breast."

I studied him for a moment, wondering if he was joking. Colin was, I guessed, in his forties. He wore a navy-blue polo shirt and jeans. He had black hair and a prominent nose and there was nothing in his expression that made me doubt him.

"So your father haunts the place?"

"I think so," Colin said. "I had a dream about him only a few months ago. He came to me and I asked him how things were on the other side. He said that they were not as he had expected but that they were okay. Then he disappeared. But this building was already haunted," Colin said. "My father is just the most recent spirit."

Colin and Nick told me the history of the building, which was over one hundred years old. Apparently at some point before the building was a bar, a girl with developmental challenges lived on the second floor. Although the exact circumstances are lost to history, the girl died in the house. It is her spirit that many believe has haunted the building for many years. There are also rumors of other ghosts haunting the pub—possibly even some connected with the 1934 shooting of gangster John Dillinger—but the misfortunate girl seems to be the most popular of them all.

"Can I go upstairs?" I asked.

"Help yourself," Colin said.

I went up the stairs across from the bar. There was no one on the second floor. A bar inlaid with black and red tiles stood at the top of the stairs. A half dozen or so small tables with captain's chairs were scattered throughout the room before a large window. Framed prints and posters hung on the cream-colored walls. One of them depicted World War II fighter planes of the Royal Air Force. I walked around for a while in the empty room, taking random photographs, trying to get a feel for whatever impressions there might have been in the place.

When the Cordwells bought the building and began renovating the second floor, workmen would frequently come back to find their tools misplaced or lost, and some of the work they had done from the day before undone even though, at the end of each day, the room would be securely locked until the following morning.

It was during these renovations that much of the ghostly activity at the pub increased, a phenomenon observed at many other haunted locations as well. It seems that ghosts don't like change. They are often roused to greater activity by physical changes in the places they knew and loved in life. Perhaps the ghosts are worried that the changes may, in some way, evict them from their eternal haunts. No ghost wants to be homeless.

If any of these nervous ghosts were following me around that day as I took pictures, I was unaware of them. I went back downstairs and left the camera with Mary, who was studying the pub's menu. We ordered some lunch and, as we waited for our order, I went back to the bar to talk with Colin and Nick.

Colin was behind the bar, putting away some glasses. Nick sat on a barstool. I sat beside him. We talked some more about John Cordwell.

"I think my father had some psychic abilities," Colin said.

He told me about his father's friend, Charlie, who had retired and moved to Florida. Colin said that one night his father dreamed about Charlie who, the elder Cordwell had said, had come to him to say good-bye. Cordwell asked where Charlie was going, but his friend did not reply. He simply disappeared.

"Later that day," Colin said, "my father got a call from someone in Florida informing him that his friend Charlie had died."

Having premonitions does not necessarily make one a psychic, nor does it guarantee ghosthood after death, but if a psychically sensitive person were surrounded by a haunted environment, such as the Red Lion pub, might that not somehow hone that person's psychic skills? Could it be something like learning a foreign language? A student learns much quicker and becomes far more proficient in that language when surrounded by native speakers. Had John Cordwell been taught by the resident ghosts the psychic tricks that would keep him tethered to this mortal plane?

As I was pondering these questions, Colin's sister Claire entered the bar. She sat by her husband Nick. Colin introduced me to her. Claire had had her share of ghostly encounters in the pub as well.

She told me that she often heard heavy footsteps thumping across the second floor when no one was there. Both Colin and Nick said they had heard them too. One night, she said, there was a loud crash from the second floor. She went upstairs and found a bar stool turned upside down, its wheels spinning. There was no one else on the second floor.

Claire was warming up to her ghost stories. She leaned across the bar and pushed her glasses up higher on her nose. She told me that she had at times "felt someone go right through me" as she sat at the bar, a phenomenon that others have felt, along with cold spots. Sudden temperature drops, forming cold spots in a certain area, are believed by some psychic investigators to be an indication of the presence of a ghost.

"But the weirdest thing was the screaming woman," Claire said.

She said that one night a woman's voice began screaming from inside the ladies' restroom on the first floor. Claire and some of the startled patrons ran to the restroom and tried to open the door. While the screaming continued from behind the door, they pushed and pulled on it but could not open it. Finally, someone called the police, who came and broke down the door.

There was no one inside.

There was no sign that anyone had been in the restroom.

The restroom had no window or any way out, other than the door. Whoever or whatever had been screaming from behind the door had simply vanished.

Was the screaming woman the ghost of the girl with developmental challenges who had lived and died in the house so many years ago?

Perhaps.

Claire recalled the night a friend of hers was conducting a CPR class in the pub. That may seem strange enough, but things got stranger. The friend went to the ladies' room and when she came back asked Claire about "the chick in the nightgown" she had seen in the restroom. Of course, when Claire and her friend checked out the restroom, it was empty, and no one in the pub had seen a woman in a nightgown entering or leaving the building.

Who was the woman in the nightgown? Was she the the girl with developmental challenges?

Claire has seen unusual figures in the pub. "I've seen something out of the corner of my eye," she said, "but I can't tell exactly what it is."

These "corner ghosts," as some researchers call them, are a common occurrence in ghosthunting. The theory is that ghosts may be visible in the infrared zones of vision, a zone not normally accessible to human vision. There is, however, an area of the eye surrounding the cornea in which humans can see at least a little into the infrared zone. Ghosts seen in this manner would appear to be viewed from the "corner" of the eye.

Whether viewed from the corner of the eye, in a photo, or as an apparition in the restroom, there is something or someone—or maybe several someones—haunting the Red Lion Pub. It's worth checking out for yourself.

North

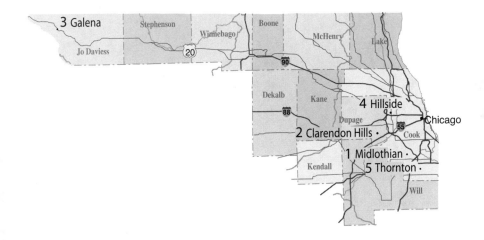

Bachelor's Grove Cemetery

MIDLOTHIAN

DESPITE ITS NAME, BACHELOR'S GROVE CEMETERY, located off Midlothian Turnpike in the southwest Chicago suburb of Midlothian, is not the eternal resting place of unmarried men. This cemetery, one of the first in the Chicago area, was most likely named for the Batchelder family, but misspelled over the years. The Batchelders were German immigrants who settled in the region in the early nineteenth century. The cemetery lies on the edge of the Rubio Woods Preserve and is not easy to find. Still, considering the fact that Bachelor's Grove Cemetery is one of the most haunted locations in the Chicago area, with more than one hundred paranormal events attributed to it, the cemetery is well worth the hunt.

My wife, Mary, and I made a visit to Bachelor's Grove on a warm day in August, armed with directions given to us by Dale Kaczmarek, noted Chicago-area psychic investigator. We easily found the Rubio Woods Preserve parking lot on the north side of 143rd Street in Midlothian and parked our car there. Across the street stood two cell towers. To their right, although not visible from our vantage point, would be the road that led into the cemetery. From where we stood in the parking lot, all we could see on the other side of the street were dense woods and tangled, weedy underbrush.

We crossed the street and walked to the right of the towers.

"Is that it?" Mary said, pointing to a rusting chain strung between two concrete posts and so overgrown with brambles and creepers as to be nearly invisible.

We could see a narrow gravel road just beyond it. There was no sign indicating the cemetery.

"I don't know," I said. "Let's check it out."

The road was rutted and littered with pieces of asphalt. We walked down the road, the dark and shadowy woods rising up on either side of us, closing over us at times like a tunnel. Narrow trails, made by animals—or perhaps, other creatures—snaked off into the murky depths of the forest. We were not that far from 143rd Street, but in the leafy confines of the forest, sounds from the outside world were lost to us. All we could hear were the scuffing of our feet on the gravel, the sigh of the wind streaming down the road, and the sudden scurrying of unknown things in the woods startled by our passing.

Several years ago, I performed a Native American vision quest, remaining alone deep in some Ohio woods for four days and four nights without food or shelter. At night, the woods grew so dark that I could not see my hand in front of my face. It was a very strange feeling, like being blind, but I did not feel uneasy or fearful. Yet, on that sunny August day, deep in the dappled woods surrounding Bachelor's Grove Cemetery, I felt a foreboding sense of melancholy, a sense of uneasiness, for which I had no rational explanation. (A few months after that visit to the cemetery, I learned that some visitors had reported seeing a red orb zipping along the trail while others had seen glowing balls of blue light. Such orbs are considered by many experts to be ghosts. We didn't see the orbs that day, but I wondered if they were what we had felt.)

About a quarter of a mile down the road, which had narrowed even more, we came to a high chain-link fence in poor condition. A wide gap in the fence allowed us to enter the cemetery.

Bachelor's Grove was like no other cemetery we had visited in the Chicago area. It was completely overgrown with weeds and tall grass. Beer cans and other debris littered the ground. Old trees dangled broken branches, while fallen limbs lay among the stones. The grave markers that had not yet been stolen or completely destroyed by vandals were broken and scattered, some half buried beneath the weeds, others desecrated with spray-painted graffiti. One huge tree felled by a storm had crashed down into the cemetery, flattening a long section of the fence beneath it. A large pond bordered one side of the cemetery, its surface completely skimmed over with pea-green algae. I would not have buried my worst enemy in such a place.

It had been at least fifty years since the last burial in Bachelor's Grove and, as time passed on, so did those who cared for the cemetery. It is an orphan now, it seems, completely abandoned by the world. Could it be that such isolation and desolation, such utter negligence by the living, have created conditions that foster a psychic environment in the cemetery that attracts ghosts? Do ghosts roam Bachelor's Grove simply because they can do so without much interference from the living?

We walked through the cemetery. Some sections of a dirt path still remained winding among the graves. Other man-made trails pushed through the weeds and grass. Mary sat in the sun on the base of a monument whose stone had disappeared while I continued exploring, taking photos as I walked.

I came across a small square stone engraved simply, Infant Daughter. It stood back to back against a much larger tombstone with the name Fulton carved upon it, but I had no idea if the two were related. So many of the stones had been moved around by vandals that it was difficult to know if this little marker actually stood above the remains of an infant girl or whether she was buried somewhere else on the grounds. Still, other visitors had commemorated the little girl's death and had left tokens of affection: a few plastic roses, a faded bead bracelet, little stuffed toys—a black cat, red teddy bear, orange teddy bear, all coming apart after being exposed to the elements. A miniature Laa-Laa of *Teletubbies* fame rested on top of the stone. It was an incredibly sad scene.

Riley Elizabeth, my first granddaughter, had been born only two months before we visited Bachelor's Grove, so it may be that I was overly sensitive at that time, but it seemed to me almost a criminal offense that the poor little nameless girl would spend eternity in a place as forlorn as that cemetery.

The thought then struck me that perhaps it was my own psychic emanations, as well as those of other visitors who were equally affected by the hopelessness and depressive nature of the cemetery, that were creating the ghosts. This was not to say that the ghosts were all "in our heads," but that maybe we were creating the psychic fuel, the energy, that ghosts needed to become manifest. This theory may help to explain the variety of ghosts seen at Bachelor's Grove.

I walked back to where Mary was sitting and told her my theory.

"Could be," she said. She looked down at the rusting Bud Light cans lying in the weeds. "Or maybe it's just the beer," she said.

She is such a skeptic.

One of the more common ghosts seen at Bachelor's Grove is that of a lady in a flowing white gown. Some have nicknamed her the "Madonna of Bachelor's Grove." She has been seen on moonlit nights walking the cemetery grounds, a baby wrapped in her arms. Is she the mother of "Infant Daughter?" At least two photos taken in the cemetery, both in broad daylight, have yielded the image of a lady in a white gown, even though she was not visible at the time the photos were taken, but appeared only as they were developed.

One of them, taken by Mari Huff, who was visiting the cemetery with members of the Ghost Research Society, shows a semi-transparent, dark-haired young woman in a white gown sitting serenely on the remains of a tombstone. Her hands lie in her lap, her feet are positioned slightly forward, and her eyes are cast downward as though she is contemplating a spot just before her. When she later saw that photo in a book, Mary reminded me that she had been sitting in exactly that same spot, apparently sitting on the ghost's lap.

The second photo shows a dark-haired young woman in a white gown just emerging from behind a tree in a wild, thickly forested part of the cemetery. She appears to be more solid than the seated woman and her gaze is turned directly toward the camera.

Neither woman carries an infant.

There are other strange ghost stories associated with the cemetery. Dale Kaczmarek tells the story of the ghost farmer in his book, *Windy City Ghosts*. According to Kaczmarek, in the late 1970s, two Cook County Forest Rangers who were on night patrol in Rubio Woods had an encounter that defied all logic. As they were approaching the pond near the cemetery, a farmer walking behind a horse-drawn plow suddenly appeared in their car's headlights. The driver of the car hit the brakes. The rangers watched in amazement as the farmer crossed the road and quickly disappeared into the darkness of the woods.

Kaczmarek's research into the event revealed that a farmer had drowned in the pond nearly a century before when the horse that was pulling his plow suddenly spooked and bolted into the pond. The farmer became entangled in the traces, was pulled into the pond with the horse, and drowned.

The scummy pond may have its own haunted history, as well. Unsubstantiated reports say that the pond was a frequent dumping place for victims of Chicago's gangland wars in the 1920s.

Mary and I had been in the cemetery only a little while when we noticed that we were not alone. A man was standing beside one of the tombstones. It seemed he appeared out of nowhere; we hadn't seen him come in, nor had we noticed him right away. He was probably in his thirties, thin, with a pale complexion and spiky blond hair. He stood quietly by the stone, studying it.

Mary nudged me. "Why don't you go over and talk with him?" she said. "See what he's doing here. Maybe he has a story for you."

This is why Mary travels with me. She feels it is her duty to prod me past my customary introverted nature, to get me to talk to strangers. I hate when she does that, especially when her prodding—a less generous husband would call it nagging—pays off.

So, I talked with him.

Greg* said that he had lived in the area all his life but had never come to the cemetery. When a friend of his who lived across town asked Greg what he knew about haunted Bachelor's Grove, Greg was embarrassed to say he knew nothing. He thought it was about time he changed that situation.

He was not a believer in ghosts, Greg said, although he did believe in spirits as they pertained to his Christian faith. We stood for some time on a narrow trail in the tall grass, talking about various theories of the afterlife. I told him about the book I was writing and he seemed interested.

All the while that we stood talking, however, I had the odd feeling that he was at the cemetery for some reason other than idle curiosity. He must have been there before we arrived, and he remained all the while we were there. Bachelor's Grove is not a large cemetery; certainly he must have seen it all long before we did. What was it he was seeking?

We went our separate ways. Every so often I would look up and find him somewhere among the weeds, gazing at the tombstones, as if he were seeing something among them that I could not see.

I concentrated on my own exploration and found myself walking down a straight dirt path through the weeds. Trees stood along the sides and broken grave markers lay partially hidden in the bushes. As I walked down the path, I noticed that there was a single gravestone at the very end, a low rectangular stone only a few feet before the chain-link fence.

I read the inscription on the stone and immediately called Mary. She came down the path and joined me.

"Look," I said, pointing to the stone.

The name Newman was carved in large letters across the face of the stone. For professional reasons, Mary uses her former surname rather than mine. That name is Newman.

Two other names were carved upon the stone in smaller letters, Daniel and Dora, husband and wife.

I would have been shaken, had I discovered my name carved on a tombstone, especially in a cemetery where probably no more than a dozen stones bore any inscription at all, but Mary seemed unperturbed.

"It's a common name," she said.

Well, sure, I thought, but to find it there, in that place, at that time? I didn't know how Mary felt, but I don't like my irony served up in cemeteries.

I took a few more photos and then we walked back toward the opening in the fence. As we left the cemetery I looked back and noticed that Greg still lingered among the graves shaded beneath the trees. I turned now and then as we walked back up the road to see if Greg was behind us, but he never appeared.

For all I know, he may still be wandering around in Bachelor's Grove Cemetery.

Country House Restaurant
CLARENDON HILLS

ON A RAINY NIGHT IN 1958 A YOUNG WOMAN
argued with the bartender at the Country House Restaurant in the
Chicago suburb of Clarendon Hills. It was obvious to other workers
who overheard their argument outside the bartender's room on the
second floor that there was something between the two, a romantic
liaison gone sour. The attractive blond woman had brought her baby
with her, a baby apparently sired by the bartender. The couple was very
angry and somehow, the young woman was pushed or fell down the
back stairs. She was stunned but not seriously injured. The distraught
woman snatched up her baby, rushed out of the restaurant into the

pouring rain, got into her car, and sped out of the lot. Less than a half mile from the restaurant, the woman's car suddenly veered, perhaps intentionally, into a telephone pole at great speed. Both the woman and her baby were killed.

From that day on, the Country House Restaurant became haunted, although it wasn't until 1974 that the ghost made herself known in a big way. Owner David Regnery was having the building renovated. As he sat at the bar with the contractor, six of the shutters over the windows suddenly flew open of their own accord, flooding the room with light. Each shutter was independently operated. There was simply no way six of them could have opened simultaneously without human assistance.

But they did.

"I remember my parents often driving by the restaurant when I was a child and telling me to look and see if I could spot the ghost," Ginny Gassen said. "They said you could see her looking out the window."

Ginny is one of the restaurant's hostesses. The night that my wife, Mary, and I had dinner there, the restaurant was busy, and she didn't have a lot of time to talk with us. Even so, she told us that she was sure strange things were happening there.

"I was so intrigued by the stories I had heard about the ghost," Ginny said, "that when this job opened up, I took it just to check it out for myself."

There wasn't much research we could do that night, with the staff rushing around as they were, tending to their customers in the crowded restaurant, so we simply enjoyed our dinner. A few days later I came back to the restaurant, this time in the morning, when I knew it would be quiet.

Brian Dodson, the Country House manager, was there to talk with me. He was tall and thin, with blondish hair. I went upstairs to the storage area and found him there. We talked just outside the door of what used to be the bartender's room and is now David Regnery's office.

"I grew up on ghost stories about the restaurant," Brian said. "My mother, Lynn, has worked here for many years, and when she came home, she used to tell me about the strange things that went on here. I can't say that I really believed her then, but I do now."

"What changed for you?" I asked.

"Over the last eight years, I've had maybe twenty people tell me about their experiences with the ghost," he said, "and they've all been similar. I started doing some research on the ghost stories and found that the stories the people told me matched what actually happened here.

"One of the weirdest people was the woman who used to live next door to the restaurant. She said that she had always had a 'problem with men' and that the ghost was just like her. In fact, she said that over the years she had often changed places with the ghost, I don't know how, and had experienced things through the ghost's eyes. Even though the woman had never been upstairs in the restaurant before, she recognized the layout and details of the second floor when she finally did visit here. That was spooky," Brian said.

One of the restaurant workers called for Brian from below and told him he had a telephone call. He told me I could look around if I liked and talk with him later.

When I was alone, I explored the rooms on the second floor. There seemed to be nothing exceptional about them. Used for storage and as the staff's "lounge," they were simply furnished and utilitarian. One large room had a couple windows that were covered with black plastic sheeting. Tall metal shelving units were pushed against the windows, covering them completely. The shelves were loaded with boxes and cans and assorted restaurant supplies. I didn't give much thought to the windows until I got my bearings and realized that the room was at the front of the building and that the windows faced the street. These were the same windows through which people outside would see a ghostly woman peering at them. The plastic sheeting and junk piled on the shelves ruled out the possibility of a real person appearing at the window and being seen by anyone outside. Even the bright light in the room could not cast a shadow through such obstacles that might be mistaken for a ghost by passers-by.

So, what was it that so many people had seen looking down at them from the window? Was it the ghost?

I walked through the room and came to the landing just above the back stairs. To my left was David Regnery's office. A few years ago Regnery had let a friend stay there for a while as the friend was going through a divorce. The man was a Clarendon Hills police officer. One night, after the restaurant had closed and everyone had gone home, the police officer was awakened by loud noises coming from outside the office door. Thinking that someone had broken into the building the man cautiously opened the door, his pistol in hand. There was no one there. He checked out the entire building, but he was alone and there was no sign that anyone had entered. He went back to sleep. The strange noises woke him up again a few nights later. Again, he found no one. After a few more nights of disturbed sleep by these ghostly sounds, the police officer moved out. Maybe he went back home, thinking that living with his estranged wife was better than living with ghosts.

The office door was locked, so I stood there quietly for a few moments, trying to imagine the events of 1958, wondering what the woman felt, trying to sense her emotional state. It was unusually quiet on the landing, as though a cone of silence had dropped down over me. The lights were on, but it seemed dimmer where I stood, almost as if a mist had collected itself there. I was roused from my reverie by a sound from the foot of the stairs.

Brian was back.

"How's it going?" He called up to me.

"All right," I said.

I started down the stairs. "Tell me something, Brian, has anyone actually seen the fight between the bartender and the woman?"

"Seen?"

"Yes, in the same way that people have seen a woman at the window." I reached the bottom and stood with him by the bar.

"Not that I know of," he said, "but there have been psychics who have come here and have gotten impressions of a woman falling down the stairs. Some of the employees have seen the ghost, but not the fight."

"They've seen the ghost?"

"Yes, some of the busboys have seen her upstairs, but the best story is about the guy who was repairing the bathroom. The guy was alone in the restaurant, doing some work in the bathroom, when he heard the jukebox come on by itself. He said it was playing music from the fifties, but there isn't any music from that time on the jukebox. He was startled by the music and when he went to check it out, he saw the figure of a woman from the waist up moving down around the bar. Then she disappeared. That freaked him out and he ran out of the restaurant and never came back."

As we talked by the bar at the rear of the main dining room, some of the wait staff was busy setting tables and getting ready for the lunch trade. Brian said that another unusual event had occurred in that dining room. He said that a local film crew had come to the restaurant to make a film about the ghost. Jennifer, one of the waitresses, was asked to play the part of the young woman because, with her blond hair, she resembled the ghost and was about the same age. Jennifer agreed.

Brian and a busboy named Geronimo were in the dining room when they saw Jennifer pull up in her car. When she walked into the room, the candle on table thirteen suddenly burst into flame; none of the candles on the other tables was lit since it was still too early in the day. There was no one else in the room before Jennifer arrived except Brian and Geronimo, and both swore they had not lit the candle. Table thirteen had already been considered by local psychics to be something of a paranormal hotspot in the restaurant, and the candle's spontaneous ignition seemed to confirm that reputation. Was table thirteen the ghost's favorite table in life?

I have been in several haunted restaurants in both Illinois and Ohio, and it seems that lighting or extinguishing candles was a favorite ghostly trick, although the point of it is lost to me. I'm still waiting for the day when some ghost reveals to us mortals the rules of the metaphysical world so that we can gain some understanding of why ghosts do the things they do.

But the candle lighting at table thirteen was just one small incident in a whole range of supernatural events occurring at the Country House Restaurant. Brian had even experienced some of them himself.

"I've heard my name called several times," Brian said, "always in a female voice, but there's never been anyone there. I've felt a hand squeeze my shoulder, only to turn around and find no one there. Other workers here have felt that same invisible hand by the way. I've even felt something unseen shoving past me on the back stairs."

The ghost stories about the restaurant have become so well known that the restaurant even includes them on its Web site. And why not? At the Country House Restaurant you can indulge both your appetite for ghosts and for the hamburgers voted "Chicago's best" by *The Chicago Tribune*. Either way, you won't be disappointed.

DeSoto House Hotel

GALENA

GALENA IS ONE OF THOSE TOWNS IN WHICH TIME has ground to a halt, and in a place like that, ghosts abound. Located in the hill country of northwestern Illinois, the town was booming in the mid-nineteenth century as a result of the lead mines (galena is the Latin word for lead sulfide) in the area. Riverboats steamed up the Mississippi River to the Galena River and to the important port of Galena, dropping off various goods and hauling away the lead. By 1850, with a population of about 6,000, Galena was one of the most important cities in what was then considered the West, along with Chicago and St. Louis. In fact, Galena's population exceeded that of Chicago.

With such prosperity it was only natural that a grand hotel be built in the city. On April 9, 1855, the DeSoto House opened for business on the corner of Main and Grand streets. It was billed as the "largest hotel in the West" and had 225 guest rooms arranged on five floors. A grand ball was held on its opening and featured a performance by Ole Bull, the famed Norwegian fiddler and musician. The hotel also boasted Ladies' Parlours, a Gentlemen's Reading Room, and a Dining Hall and Carving Room one hundred feet long that could seat three hundred people. In 1858, diners could order a dinner of roast steer and suet pudding for forty cents, or perhaps a native bear steak with elderberry jelly for fifty-five cents, although at thirty cents the baked wild turkey with corn bread stuffing was a real bargain.

The good citizens of Galena were so impressed by their own success that they failed to see the warning signs of impending disaster before them. By 1870 the lead mines were losing commercial importance, due to increased mining costs and newer mines discovered farther west. In addition, many of Galena's leading citizens had their money tied up in riverboat companies and other river-based industries and ignored the growth of railroads. When the Illinois Central Railroad wanted to build a bridge across the Galena River, these prominent citizens opposed it, fearing it would interfere with river traffic. As a result, the railroad located its new western terminus on the west bank of the Mississippi River in Dunleith, now known as East Dubuque, Iowa. The commerce and wealth that rode the railroads bypassed Galena.

Hezekiah Gear, who was himself a wealthy mine owner and steamboater knew the consequences of turning down the railroad. "Gentlemen," he said, "you have sounded your death knell, grass will grow in your streets, you have ruined your town."

To make matters worse, the erosion of the hillsides caused by the lead mining dumped tons of silt into the Galena River, choking the channel, eventually making it unnavigable to riverboats. The town had strangled itself.

The economic bust in Galena affected the DeSoto House as well. In its heyday, it had seen the likes of Abraham Lincoln, who made a speech there in 1856 in support of Republican presidential candidate John C. Fremont. Lincoln's own adversary for the U.S. Senate, Stephen Douglas, spoke from the hotel's balcony in 1858. Perhaps its proudest moment was when the hotel hosted the 1865 homecoming of one of Galena's most famous residents, General Ulysses S. Grant. More than 25,000 people thronged the streets that day and a triple-arched viewing stand spanned Main Street in front of the hotel. The Grand Reception Ball at the hotel that evening in honor of General Grant drew 2,000 people. Grant later launched his 1868 campaign for the presidency from the hotel. Other notable visitors to DeSoto House in the late nineteenth century included Dorothea Dix, General George McClellan, William Jennings Bryan, and Tom Thumb. Still, hard times came calling at the hotel.

In 1859 a fire nearly destroyed the hotel and in 1869 a boiler exploded in a dye works that had leased space in the hotel's basement. The explosion was so powerful that the main head of the boiler was thrown across the street and into a grocery, smashing through its door, and nearly taking the head off a man, while the boiler itself took the opposite direction, knocking out holes eight feet in diameter through two brick walls, each a foot thick. Parts of the boiler flew straight up through the floor above and into Chris Plaith's billiard hall, scattering fragments everywhere, propelling the heavy billiard tables up off the floor. The boiler explosion fatally scalded Christian Struber, the owner of the dye works.

Could such a horrible death be linked to the ghosts that float through the corridors of the hotel? That was the question I asked Scott Wolfe.

Scott, who was considered the hotel's resident historian, was seated behind the high front desk counter the day I investigated the hotel. A thin man with blond hair and matching Van Dyke, he looked more like a U.S. Cavalry officer or perhaps an Old West lawman. In fact, there was something of the Old West in the décor of DeSoto House. The floor was carpeted in an ornate floral pattern, and the walls were papered in a different but equally ornate pattern. A beautiful white pressed-tin ceiling was overhead and behind me a graceful wood-carved staircase curved up to the second floor. A large floral arrangement stood upon a wooden stand near a marble-topped table and a velvet-upholstered parlor chair.

Scott had collected ghost stories about the hotel, although he declined to identify any of the ghosts. There was just no way of knowing who they were, he said, considering the thousands of people who had come and gone since the hotel first opened its doors in 1855.

Scott told me that guests have seen misty figures walking in the halls and walking through the walls, especially on the second and third floors on the hotel's southern and southeastern sides. Guests have also wakened in the middle of the night to see a ghostly figure standing at the foots of their beds.

"The hotel has been reconfigured a few times over the course of its history," Scott said, "and it may be that when a ghost walks through a wall, it is actually walking through a doorway that existed in its own time, when it was alive, but that no longer exists."

Such remodeling or renovation is frequently cited as an explanation for why ghosts seem to walk through walls. Some psychic researchers also believe that renovating a building stirs up the ghosts, maybe because they feel they are somehow being evicted from their home, or maybe because they simply don't like change. That could be what happened at DeSoto House, which went through a $7.8 million restoration completed in 1986. There were other, earlier changes too. Besides the renovations necessitated by the 1859 fire, the top two floors of the hotel were removed in 1880 due to lack of business. Captain Asa Haile, who had directed the original construction of the hotel, had the roof jacked up, tore out the two floors, then resettled the same roof on the remaining floors. A lot of dust has been stirred up at the hotel with these changes and, no doubt, a few ghosts as well.

"Some of the ghosts seem to come from the Civil War era," Scott said. "Guests have seen men in uniform and ladies in hoop skirts."

He told me about the mother and daughter who had seen the same ghost when they were guests at the hotel. The mother was lying awake in bed and the daughter was sitting in a chair. The daughter looked up and saw a woman in a hoop skirt standing in front of the window.

Before she could call to her mother, the ghost vanished.

The girl turned to her mother. "Did you see what I saw?" she asked, afraid to give voice to the word ghost.

"Yes," her mother said, "I saw it too."

After speaking with Scott, I had lunch in The Courtyard, one of the hotel's three restaurants. The Courtyard was an open atrium surrounded on four sides by guest rooms. As is my habit, I spoke with two of the waitresses there, Kim Basten and Carrie Williams, and asked them if they had had any contact with the hotel's ghosts. Kim was new at the hotel and listened attentively while Carrie told what she knew of the ghosts.

Carrie repeated the same stories that Scott had told me about ghosts walking through walls. Although she had not seen them herself, Carrie told us that some members of the housekeeping staff had seen ghosts.

"They've seen these figures flitting around in the halls," she said.

When I asked her where they had been seen, Carrie indicated an area that matched the locations on the second and third floors that Scott had given.

"What did they look like?" I asked.

"You know," Carrie said, "just ghostly."

Indeed.

The sleepy town of Galena has roused itself from slumber. It has been rediscovered, this time for its old architecture, historic buildings, and trendy shops and boutiques, and has become a get-away-from-it-all destination for visiting Chicagoans. Unfortunately for them, but happily for you, the ghosts of the DeSoto House Hotel have nowhere else to "get away from it all."

Galena/Jo Daviess County Historical Society and Museum

GALENA

THE GALENA/JO DAVIESS COUNTY HISTORICAL society and museum is housed in an elegant Italianate-style home built in 1858 by wealthy Galena businessman Daniel Barrows. The building sits on Bench Street, just a few doors down from haunted Turner Hall, and is itself the home of a ghost or two.

Daryl Watson is the museum's curator, and he has written about the ghosts at the museum and at other sites in Galena in his book, *Ghosts of Galena.* Daryl was in a meeting when I arrived at the museum, so I had the opportunity to look around by myself for a while.

I stood in the brown-and-white-tiled entry hall admiring the gracefully curved staircase leading up to the second floor. A small marble bust of a man sat in a niche in the wall at the top of the stairs. I walked into the room at the right of the entry foyer and found myself in the museum's gift shop. The ornate crown molding of the room hinted at a more gracious use in times gone by, perhaps the scene of a fancy dinner party hosted by Daniel Barrows and his wife for Galena's elite.

Ted*, the friendly volunteer working in the gift shop, was not at all shy when it came to talking about ghosts. "Galena's full of them," he said. "My own house is haunted."

I had heard plenty about the ghosts of Galena during the days that my wife, Mary, and I visited the town and wondered if perhaps there were not some reasonable explanations for them. Mary is an expert in occupational safety and health and knows a thing or two about lead poisoning, including the fact that excessive exposure to the element can cause madness, and where there is madness, there is also the potential for mayhem and murder, trauma that can produce ghosts. It should come as no surprise that Galena, once a center for lead mining, also contained an asylum for the insane.

But Ted was not insane, at least not that I could tell. He seemed reasonable and, well, normal. Still, his house was haunted and he was okay with that. I asked him about the museum ghosts.

"I've never seen them," Ted said, "but people say they hear footsteps when there is no one around, or just have the sense that something is there watching them. I've felt that too. Daryl has a lot more stories he can tell you."

I went across the hall with a few other visitors and watched a slide show about the history of Galena, then wandered upstairs. The museum was not very large but was interesting. One room was dedicated to the town's steamboating history while a larger room held displays related to the town's mining history, as well as exhibits about regional Native Americans. In one section was a small display of personal items owned by Galena's best-known resident, General Ulysses S. Grant, as well as leather goods from the Grant family store.

In a corner of the mining exhibit area was a model lead mine. I stood in a little alcove and looked straight down through the window into a realistic mine shaft. In the gloom below me was a lifelike mannequin hard at work. I half expected the miner to raise his head and look up at me.

I had read Daryl's book before visiting the museum. He had written that the ghostly happenings at the museum began in 1988 when a piano on the ground floor played a chord by itself as a female museum employee walked by. In the spring of 1989, mysterious footsteps were heard so often walking in the halls and up and down stairs that museum employees began recording paranormal events on a computer. More footsteps. Rapping on the walls. The sound of furniture being moved around. A chandelier that began swinging of its own accord.

In January 1990, a male employee walked down stairs, his heart pounding as he heard footsteps shuffling down the stairs behind him. When he got to the ground floor, he felt the footsteps move right through him out into the hall, where he heard what sounded like a shoe sliding across the tiled floor.

One of the most bizarre events recorded at the museum occurred during a VIP reception in January 1991. The reception was a catered affair. One of the servers inexplicably dropped an entire tray of glasses filled with champagne. Ten minutes later another server watched helplessly as the glasses on her tray suddenly began to shake, then crashed to the floor, along with the tray. A third tray sitting on a counter in the gift shop began to tremble, spilling half of the glasses onto the floor. As three servers lined up with glass-filled trays, one of the trays began to shake. The server grabbed it firmly in both hands, saying, "Oh, shit, I don't believe this!" but most of the glasses toppled anyway.

I was aware of these past events as I meandered through the museum and would pause now and then in some still corner, waiting to see if anything would make itself known. Nothing did.

Daryl Watson had concluded his meeting and asked me into his office. Daryl was a thin, quiet man, the kind you would expect to find working at a museum or library and he sat silently behind his desk as I explained why I was in Galena and, more precisely, why I was visiting the museum. I expected a comrade-in-arms reaction from him. After all, he had written about the ghosts of Galena and had apparently lived with them at the museum. He was cordial but circumspect.

"Those events took place several years ago," he said, "over a course of only a few short years. The museum has been quiet since then."

I took quiet to mean not haunted. I asked him to elaborate on the stories he had told in his book, but he declined, remarking that all he had to say he had said in the book. Again, polite, but not exactly forthcoming. It seemed to me that I was getting a brushoff, and I wondered if perhaps other people connected to the historical society had not reacted well to Daryl's stories about the museum being haunted, and had told him so. My little talk with Ted in the gift shop left me with the clear impression that the museum was not as quiet as Daryl would have me believe.

"There's nothing going on now," Daryl insisted.

That could be, I thought, as I shook hands with him and walked out of the office, but I remembered that Daryl himself had written about a weird incident that occurred at the museum forty years ago, when the Galena City Hall was located in the building. A city council meeting was interrupted by a loud commotion from upstairs, but when the mayor and councilmen rushed upstairs to see what was going on, they found nothing disturbed and no one there.

It is possible, of course, that the ghosts of Galena's History Museum have departed for other paranormal digs, but it is equally possible that they are simply taking a breather, ready to come back another day. Time will tell.

Turner Hall
GALENA

THE MID-NINETEENTH CENTURY SAW A RISE OF social organizations among immigrants to America dedicated to helping their fellow countrymen succeed in their adopted country while simultaneously fostering their ethnic cultures. One such group was the Turner Society, which flourished among German-Americans, especially in the Midwest, where German populations were high. The first Turner Society was founded in Cincinnati, Ohio, in 1848 and by 1851, there were so many societies established across the country that a national organization, the North American Turner

Association (Turnerbund) was set up to oversee them. The Turner Society philosophy was based upon the idea of a "sound mind in a sound body." Turner Societies built gymnasiums, music and lecture halls, and libraries throughout the country, and provided classes that fed the body, such as physical fitness, nutrition, and health, as well as offerings for the mind in music, literature, art, and the study of the German language. Thousands of German-Americans took advantage of the Turner Society to help them find community among their kinsmen and to help them achieve economic and social success in America. The Cincinnati Turner Settlement Society founded the town of New Ulm, Minnesota, in 1854 and during the Civil War, the Turners composed the entire 9th Ohio Voluntary Infantry Regiment.

The Turner Society in Galena built its own Turner Hall in 1874. Since its founding, the hall has hosted innumerable performances and public assemblies of various kinds and continues to this day, over a century later.

Turner Hall also hosts a few ghosts who have been known to give eerie performances of their own.

From the outside Turner Hall looks something like a castle on the Rhine. Built from sandy-colored limestone block, the building sits on a slight hill on Bench Street, right beside the fire department. The central section of the hall has a porthole window high in its apex. Three long, arched windows with a balcony grace the façade. Each wing of the hall has its own set of arched windows and double doors with fanlight windows above them. Stone steps lead up to the imposing doors of the main entrance. Wrought-iron lanterns frame the doors. Imposing by day, Turner Hall could look absolutely terrifying on a dark, moonless night.

Inside, Turner Hall is less foreboding, although it is still like stepping back in time. The wood floors are polished and gleam in the low light from wall sconces scattered throughout the hall. The walls are painted white and cream and make the space seem larger than it is. The stage is trimmed in dark wood and that same wood is used in the columns and balustrades of the curved wings on either side of the stage. There is a balcony at the rear of the hall with rows of wooden seats, the kind one might find in an old ballpark. Standing on the floor, looking up into the gloom of the balcony, it seemed entirely conceivable that ghosts could still reside there.

No one knows for sure who the spirit is, if indeed it is only one person, that haunts Turner Hall, but many suspect it is Charles Scheerer. A furniture maker and part-time undertaker, Scheerer was active with the Turner Society and served as its treasurer. He spent many years managing the hall and watching over it; he even lived his last day on earth in the hall. On March 14, 1910, his body was found lying on the floor of Turner Hall, dead from natural causes. Could it be that Charles Scheerer still watches over his beloved hall?

In 1991, a local minister and his daughter were alone in Turner Hall, setting up a projector in the balcony, when they suddenly heard an angry male voice. They could not tell exactly what the voice was saying but the tone was unmistakable. The minister looked around to see who had spoken to them, but there was no one to be seen. He and his daughter went back to working on the projector when the voice spoke up again. For fifteen to twenty seconds, the angry but unintelligible voice growled at them. This time, they left their work undone and fled the hall.

On another occasion two women, volunteers from the Save Turner Hall organization, were standing backstage in the hall when they felt a blast of icy air sweep over them. They stepped out of the draft and no sooner had they moved from that spot, than a stone crashed to the floor where they had been standing. The stone had come loose from high up on the wall behind them and surely would have struck one of them had they not moved. Was the Turner Hall ghost trying to protect them or scare them away with a warning?

Other volunteers who were working to renovate and preserve Turner Hall also had ghostly experiences there. One night four of them were building sets on stage when they saw someone walk past the dressing room door. Of course, there was no one there when they checked out the dressing room. Another time a volunteer working in the attic turned off the light as he was about to leave. In the second before the attic went dark, he was sure he saw someone in the room with him. Quickly he flicked the light back on, his heart pounding, but the bright light revealed only what he already knew; he was alone in the attic.

Around Halloween 2003, *Galena Gazette* editor Jay Dickerson was looking for ideas for a holiday feature. A skeptic about things paranormal, Jay decided to spend a night alone in Turner Hall to find out for himself whether or not ghosts stalk the hall. I stopped in to visit with him at his office at the newspaper to hear about his experiences at Turner Hall.

Jay was a young guy with a full beard and a winning smile. He seemed to me as reasonable and rational as a newspaper editor should be. He said that his original idea was to spend the entire night alone at Turner Hall, armed with a 35mm camera, a digital camera, video camera, and tape recorder.

"Original?" I said, "Did your plans change?"

"Yes. My wife was expecting with our second child, and she didn't want me to be away all night, so I had to shorten my stay at the hall."

"How long were you there?"

"Long enough to order a pizza," Jay said.

Jay got to the hall at about 4 p.m., set up his equipment in various locations inside, and sat and waited. Every so often, he would get up and make the rounds, checking on his equipment. Nothing unusual happened during these rounds. Night came on but the hall was quiet.

"It was pretty boring, really," Jay said. "Just about midnight, I decided that I should probably get home to my wife. I packed up all my gear, made one last check throughout the building, turned off the lights and hauled all my stuff out the front door. I closed the door behind me and locked it and just as I did that, something banged loudly several times on the other side of the door."

"Did you go back inside?" I asked.

"No way," Jay said. "Whatever it was, though, had a real good sense of humor."

Jay used to say that he was "kind of up in the air" about whether or not ghosts were real. These days, he's a believer.

Mount Carmel Cemetery

HILLSIDE

THERE ARE PROBABLY MORE DEAD ITALIANS IN Mount Carmel Cemetery than there are in Rome. This sprawling cemetery on Chicago's West Side was, and remains, a favorite and fashionable place of eternal repose for many of Chicagoland's Italian-American families. Beneath the manicured lawns lie the remains of simple working people, as well as illustrious citizens and high-ranking members of the Catholic clergy. These good folk share the sod with some less reputable men. Al Capone and his enforcer, Frank Nitti, are just two of them.

I was fortunate enough to be visiting Mount Carmel with Dale Kaczmarek, a well-known paranormal researcher and founder and president of the Ghost Research Society located in the Chicago suburb of Oak Lawn. Dale is a lifelong resident of the Chicago area and knows its history, both actual and paranormal, better than anyone else.

"Capone's grave is hard to find," Dale said, as I drove down one of the cemetery roads. "It's right in plain sight, but people miss it all the time."

I had entered the cemetery through the main gate at Roosevelt Road and driven down the first road on the right as Dale directed.

"Stop here," Dale said, after I had gone probably no more than one hundred yards. "That's it." He nodded toward a tall grave marker bearing a sculpted cross. Dense shrubs were planted at the foot of the stone and obscured the bottom half, including the name Capone engraved upon it. A wrought-iron fence ran behind the stone. Beyond the fence, cars and buses whooshed up and down Roosevelt Road.

We got out of the car, Dale moving more slowly than me since he was dragging around a cast on his right foot, a result of an injury at the frozen food plant at which he worked. It didn't help that his six-foot frame was folded somewhat uncomfortably in the passenger seat of the Mitsubishi I was driving. I made a mental note to rent larger cars in the future, or hang out with shorter investigators.

Even as we stood directly before the monument, the family name was invisible, completely hidden behind the dense evergreens. Dale thought that maybe the groundskeepers had let the shrubs grow to cover the name in order to discourage crowds of the curious, people like Dale and me.

In the grass before the marker, however, were several rectangular stones set at ground level, each engraved with the name of a Capone family member. One of the simple granite markers read: Alphonse Capone, 1899 – 1947, My Jesus Mercy. Other visitors had left a few coins and a burnt-out stogie on his stone.

I asked Dale if there were any ghost stories associated with Capone's grave. He said there were not, but he did tell me how Capone was terrorized, and some say, driven insane by a ghostly visitor while he was incarcerated in Alcatraz for tax evasion. Capone swore to friends and family members that the ghost of James Clark, one of the men gunned down in the infamous 1929 St. Valentine's Day Massacre ordered by Capone, haunted him. He claimed that Clark had been haunting him ever since he was murdered. In time, Capone was reduced to a frightened shell of his former self, a man who often refused to leave his cell and constantly mumbled to himself. When he was released in 1939, he was too unstable mentally to take control of his gang again. His insanity was most likely caused by his advanced case of syphilis, but right up until the time of his death in 1947, Capone believed that the ghost of James Clark was tormenting him.

Only a short distance from Capone's grave is the grave of his enforcer, Frank Nitti. The monument is easy to spot and is engraved Nitto, the family's preferred spelling of their name. An ornate cross is carved into the tall monument.

After serving Capone faithfully for many years, Nitti died in 1943, not in a gangland slaying as was so common for Chicago mobsters of that era, but by his own hand. One evening in March he took a walk along the Illinois Central Railroad tracks near Harlem and Cermak avenues, a gun in his pocket. At some point, as he walked down the tracks, Nitti pulled out the pistol, pointed it at his head and fired. Nearby railroad workers heard the shot and looked up to see a man standing on the tracks holding a smoking gun near his head. Incredibly, Nitti's first shot had missed. His second shot did not. He pitched face down on the tracks, dead.

It is said that Frank Nitti still haunts the spot where he killed himself. Several people have reported spotting a mysterious figure walking along the tracks. Some have seen it stagger and fall before disappearing completely.

Yet, as interesting as these stories were, Dale and I had come to Mount Carmel Cemetery not in search of gangland ghosts but to see the Italian Bride. We drove around to the Harrison Street side of the cemetery and parked across the road from the monument to Julia Buccola Peta. A life-sized statue of Julia stands atop a large stone. She is dressed in a long, sweeping wedding gown and wears a lace cap with a veil. She cradles a large bouquet of roses in her arms. The statue is modeled after a photo of the bride taken on her wedding day. That photo is rendered in porcelain on the stone beneath her feet.

A second, more macabre porcelain photo is set in the stone below the first photo. This photo depicts the body of Julia lying in her open coffin six years after her burial. Despite the loose dirt around the coffin and the stains upon the satin lining inside it, Julia's body is fresh and uncorrupted. She looks merely asleep, certainly not dead and buried for six years. An Italian inscription engraved upon the stone reads, "Questa fotografia presa dopo 6 anni morta." A loose translation would be: "What is this photograph taken six years after her death?"

That's what I wanted to know, as did the four elderly women who were gathered before the monument when we arrived. They had read the inscription and studied the photos, but were confused about the real story of poor Julia.

"Do either of you know her story?" one of the women asked us, after we had crossed the road and exchanged greetings.

"Wasn't she buried alive by mistake?" one of the women asked.

Dale stumped around to the front of the monument. Dale conducts haunted tours of Chicago and knows all the stories, including that of the Italian Bride. He was on stage now.

According to Dale, Julia Buccola Peta died in 1921 from a raging fever, a complication of childbirth. She was only 29 years old; her baby was delivered stillborn. Mother and child were buried, Julia dressed in her wedding gown, a Sicilian tradition for mothers who die in childbirth. They were laid to rest beneath a simple grave marker.

Julia's mother, Philomena Buccola, was, understandably, heartbroken. Shortly after her daughter died, Philomena began having troubling dreams in which Julia appeared to her and begged to have her body exhumed. There was no reason for Philomena to believe that her daughter's death had been anything other than a tragic medical event, but the dream persisted. Julia persisted.

"The dreams went on for several years," Dale said, "and Philomena became convinced, that for whatever reason, she must exhume the body of her daughter. She went to the authorities to try to get an order for exhumation, but the Catholic diocese that ran the cemetery wasn't willing to allow it."

The authorities were reluctant, in the absence of any legal reasons, to exhume the body, but Philomena, convinced that her daughter was trying to tell her something from beyond the grave, was stubborn in her resolve. She continued to petition the diocese and finally, in 1927, permission was granted to exhume Julia's body.

As Philomena and other family members stood by, the gravediggers dug up the coffin and placed it on the grass. It was stained and worn, as would be expected after six years in the ground. Two of the men opened the lid. There lay Julia in peaceful repose, her face as fresh as it had been in life, her dark curly hair looking as though she had brushed it only a few minutes before, her wedding gown and veil immaculate.

Someone took the famous photo that now graces Julia's monument. Philomena's reaction to the state of her daughter's body has been lost to history, but she must have been satisfied by what she saw. Julia was once again sealed up inside her coffin and was reburied. The elaborate monument that now marks her burial site was erected, the two photos reproduced in porcelain upon the base.

There is a tradition in Catholicism of saints' bodies remaining incorruptible long after their deaths, and rumors soon spread that Julia must be a saint. Why else would her body have remained free from corruption? Despite her incorruptibility, however, none of the traditional miracles associated with saints were ever attributed to Julia.

As Dale explained to the women, Julia's story does not end here.

Saint or not, it is said that Julia's spirit still walks among the tombstones of Mount Carmel Cemetery. The figure of a girl has often been seen flitting through the cemetery after dark. One rainy night, near Halloween of course, a group of people driving in a car on Harrison Street were startled to see a woman walking among the graves. They stopped the car to get a better look. Perhaps, it was a prankster, they thought. After all, it was late at night, and it was almost Halloween. The figure was probably no more than thirty feet away when they noticed that, despite the downpour, the woman was absolutely dry. Not a hair on her head out of place. No sopping wrinkles in her dress. That was enough to convince the people that what they had seen was no prankster.

Dale also said that at least one person has seen Julia's monument glowing at night and others have reported the scent of fresh roses at her grave, even in the winter, when it was unlikely such fragrances would occur naturally.

If Julia's mortal remains are truly incorruptible, then what of her spiritual remains? If her perfectly preserved body lies beneath the grass of Mount Carmel Cemetery, is it so difficult to believe that her perfectly preserved spirit still walks among us?

Widow McCleary's Pub & Grill

THORNTON

I GREW UP IN NEW ENGLAND, WHERE "GEORGE Washington Slept Here" signs are so ubiquitous as to make you think our first president was narcoleptic. In the Chicago area, it's Al Capone whose legend as our nation's first weapon of mass destruction is written large. There should be signs saying, "Al Capone Rubbed Someone Out Here." No doubt, one of those signs would be prominently displayed at Widow McCleary's Pub & Grill in the southeastern Chicago suburb of Thornton.

Widow McCleary's is a two-story brick building with large windows overlooking a parking lot that was half-filled with pickup trucks and motorcycles on the day I stopped by. Built in 1876 by German immigrant John S. Bielfeldt, the building maintained some of the decorative brickwork and trim of that time. Bielfeldt drilled an artesian well for the brewery he operated out of the building so that only pure, clean water from a nearby creek went into his beer. That well still bubbles up deep beneath the building. Around the turn of the nineteenth century, Bielfeldt handed over the brewery to one of his longtime employees, Sean Patrick McCleary.

During the Prohibition era, McCleary continued to operate the brewery illegally. One night he was visited by Al Capone, who was interested in going into business with McCleary. The brewer refused Capone's partnership "offer" and only a few days later, a mysterious fire broke out at the brewery. McCleary and several of his workers disappeared and were presumed burned to death in the fire. McCleary's widow, Margaret Mary, was in no position to refuse Capone a second time. He took over the brewery and ran part of his bootlegging operations out of it, far from the eyes of the Chicago Police Department and the FBI.

There was nothing reminiscent of those violent days when I visited Widow McCleary's. As I walked up the stairs to the large deck outside the pub, a motorcycle roared up behind me driven by a bald, middle-aged man with a white goatee and moustache. He wore jeans and a T-shirt, no helmet—not on a Harley. He looked like he belonged to the Burl Ives Chapter of the Hell's Angels.

I went inside and entered a small, square room. It barely allowed space for the bar around which half a dozen men sat smoking and drinking. Behind the bar, a young woman in jeans and T-shirt kept their glasses filled. Framed photos and copies of old newspapers recounting the exploits of Al Capone and other Chicagoland mobsters hung on the walls. One of the photos depicted the smoking ruins of the brewery after the fire attributed to Capone. By the door was a carved and painted staircase. In the stairwell hung a picture of John S. Bielfeldt.

I walked up to the bar. Mindy, the bartender, greeted me with a smile and asked what I wanted. I told her I was interested in the ghost stories and asked her if she knew any. In almost any other setting such a question would have generated a strange look and, no doubt, an unprintable response, but not at Widow McCleary's.

"Oh, yes, there are plenty of stories here," Mindy said. "I've never experienced the ghost myself but my husband has. Go on, Tad, tell him what happened," she said to one of the men seated at the bar.

Tad had longish hair and wore a black Harley-Davidson T-shirt. He looked up from his beer, but didn't want to talk. "You tell it," he said to his wife.

Mindy wasted no time. She told me that late one night, as the bar was about to close, Tad heard a deep sigh beside him where he sat at the bar.

"It was right in his ear," Mindy said, "but there was no one there. Then he saw a bright flash of light beside him. It nearly knocked him off his bar stool, he was so scared."

I sat at the bar while she told the story. Just as Mindy was finishing her story, another bartender entered the room and stood by me.

"Did you tell him about the little girl?" she asked. Before Mindy could answer, the woman seated herself on the stool beside me and started in with her story. The woman's name was Grace Poort. She had been on her way home, but talk of the ghost made her linger.

"We think there are a few ghosts here," she said, lighting up a cigarette. "There's a mean one down here that likes to hang out by the ice machine and upstairs there's a lady and a little girl. The little girl likes to play with the balls from the pool table.

"The mean one likes to pull hair. He even pulled the backs of my earrings off one time. He throws stuff, too. He used to throw glasses and things at one of our bartenders, Moe's niece," she said.

"Moe?"

"The owner," Grace said, blowing out a puff of smoke. "That's him there." She nodded toward a man who had just entered the bar. It was the Burl Ives look-alike.

I introduced myself and we shook hands. Moe Birkenfeld was just there to have a quick lunch before heading off on some other business, but he was willing to talk about the ghosts.

"Yeah, the ghost just didn't like my niece at all," he said, with a laugh. "It got so bad, she quit."

"Any idea who this ghost is?" I asked.

He shook his head. "Not really, could be one of Al Capone's victims, maybe. Who knows? Back in the fifties, this building was being renovated and ten bodies were discovered buried in the walls."

"Was that McCleary and the others who disappeared in the fire?" I asked.

"No one knows," Grace said.

"The owner at that time reburied the bodies," Moe said.

"He was Italian," Grace said. My own Sicilian heritage caused me to suspect she meant something by that remark, although I was not certain exactly what.

"No one knows where they were buried," Moe added. "You should talk to my wife, Sharon. She can tell you a lot of this stuff."

As if on cue, Sharon came from out of the kitchen to the bar carrying plates of sandwiches for Moe and herself. She was a tall blond woman, the cutoff shorts she wore making her seem even taller. I decided to let Sharon and Mo have their lunch in peace and asked if I could look around.

"No problem," Sharon said.

"I can take you upstairs if you want," Grace said. "We can see if the little girl ghost wants to play."

Sure, I thought, we could do that, and then maybe later, we could all go bowling with Casper the Friendly.

I followed Grace upstairs. One half of the large second-floor room was set up as a dining room with a dozen or so tables arranged before large windows, each fringed with a blue-checkered curtain. The other side of the room had a long bar, several bar stools, cocktail tables, and a pool table in the center. A sign over the bar read, If our barmaids look beautiful, don't drive.

"Let's see if she wants to play," Grace said, taking the cue ball off the pool table.

She stood by the wall about eight feet away from me and placed the ball on the wood floor. It began to roll slowly in my general direction.

"We'll see if she likes you," Grace said.

"How do you know it's a girl?" I asked.

"It's just a feeling we all have, all us women, especially Sharon Junior."

"Who's that?"

"She's another one of the bartenders. We call her 'Junior' to tell her apart from the other Sharon, Moe's wife. Junior comes up here a lot and plays with the ghost, more than anybody else."

The cue ball was still rolling but now it curved in its path so that it was heading right for me. Just a foot or so away from me it slowed and came to a stop

"She's checking you out," Grace said, lighting another cigarette.

After a few seconds the ball began to move again, this time to my left.

"If she likes you, she'll roll the ball in a circle around you," Grace said.

The ball did start to arc around me, but then turned in and came to rest against the tip of my shoe.

"I guess she doesn't want to play today," Grace said.

No sooner had she said those words, than the ball backed away from my foot and started to roll in the opposite direction it had come. All right, I thought, these are wood floors. Very old, warped, and probably not level. Of course the ball would roll on its own.

"Let's try again," Grace said, picking up the ball and setting it back down again by the wall. At first it ran in a straight line toward the other side of the room. "That's just the floor itself doing that," Grace said, admitting what I had suspected. "These floors are pretty uneven."

But then the ball came to a complete stop, rested for a second, then rolled back on itself, stopped, rolled to the left in a little circle, stopped, rolled right again, then forward, before finally finding a warped dip in the floor that sent it speeding the rest of the way across the room.

Grace was disappointed. "She just wasn't in a playful mood today, I guess."

Still, I saw that cue ball move in ways that I could not explain. Old floors or not, that ball was doing tricks.

We went back downstairs. Sharon was still at the bar, but Moe was gone.

"Did she want to play?" Sharon asked.

"Not much," Grace said.

"She really likes it when Sharon Junior's here," Sharon said.

Sharon asked if I wanted to see some ghost photos taken there. She went to the kitchen and returned with a manila envelope that she placed on the bar.

"These were taken upstairs," she said, opening the envelope and drawing out the photos.

I sat at the bar, Sharon on one side of me, Grace on the other, both women puffing on cigarettes, and examined the photos. Round balls of hazy white light appeared in some of them, floating by the bar.

Many psychic researchers believe that a camera can sometimes capture ghosts, invisible to the naked eye, on film. These ghosts will only become apparent when the film is developed or, in the case of digital cameras, when the image is downloaded onto the computer. Sometimes the ghosts appear as misty streaks or swirls, but more commonly, they appear as whitish orbs, like those in Sharon's photos.

In addition to the orbs, one of the photos also depicted, according to the women, three ghostly faces near the pool table, although, try as I might, I just couldn't see them. This has got to be some physical failing on my part—I do have terrible vision—since I so often am unable to see the ghost faces that people point out to me in their photographs. My wife, Mary, has suggested that I get some additional occupational training by studying cloud formations.

"We don't know who these ghosts are," Grace said. "Maybe they're the ghosts of the people who were dug up here in the fifties."

"It's really too bad we don't know where they were reburied," Sharon added.

I thought of the old artesian well that was used by the brewery and wondered aloud if that might not be a likely spot, wherever it was. Sharon agreed and said that there were stories about some of the bodies being discovered there.

"Could I see the well?" I asked.

Sharon stubbed out her cigarette in an ashtray. "I don't think it's padlocked anymore. Let me see if I can find a flashlight."

She left the bar, went back to the office, and returned shortly with a flashlight. I followed her out of the bar, down the steps off the deck and out into the parking lot. We walked over to a one-story wing that extended off the main building. With some effort Sharon pulled open a solid metal door and we entered a dusty, dirty room that looked like it may have been some kind of machine shop or storage area. On the back wall was a low, arched doorway. Beyond the door lay a tunnel, the walls and ceiling made of stone blocks damp with moisture, stained with mold. A second doorway at the end of the tunnel led only to darkness.

"This is it," Sharon said. "I better lead since I have the light and know my way around down here. Watch your step, there's a slope."

I ducked my head under the arch as I followed Sharon into the tunnel. By the time we passed through the second doorway, we were in complete darkness. We descended some sort of ramp, the floor rough and uneven beneath my feet. The air was cool and damp. I could feel the currents of air sliding by me palpable as some cave creature startled by our light. Sharon's flashlight, however, didn't illuminate much. All I could see in the dark was her white tennis shoes moving ahead of me; I assumed the rest of her was attached to them.

"Careful," Sharon said as we scuffed along in the dank tunnel.

After walking a little more I saw her shoes come to a stop and was able to stop before crashing into her.

"Here it is," Sharon said.

I stood beside her as she played the flashlight around the room. The light revealed the tunnel with its low barrel-vaulted roof, a solid wall before us. In the dim light, the stones were gray and glistening wet. It was as though we had wandered into an Edgar Allan Poe story. A cube maybe three feet square and made of bricks stood in the center of the room. It was layered with dust and dirt from many years. A narrow pipe protruded from the front of the cube. The bricks below the pipe were water-stained.

"The well is dry now," Sharon said, moving the light over the brick cube and the pipe, "but you never know. Sometimes this tunnel is actually flooded. There's usually some water in here."

As her light continued to sweep the room, I noticed at least one area in the wall where the bricks had been disturbed and replaced, leaving a discolored square imprinted upon the wall. I wondered what was beyond that square. Could that be where the bodies were found? Was it where they were reburied? Sharon didn't know, but I thought that dark and hidden tunnel seemed like an excellent place to hide a corpse, even though I didn't have any firsthand experience in that regard.

As we started to leave the tunnel, I asked Sharon if she would go on ahead to the entrance to the tunnel and let me stay behind in the dark to take some pictures. She moved off, her light growing dimmer as she went.

I was literally shooting in the dark as I took the photos and each flash was like lightning in the small room, unidentifiable objects and strange shadows leaping out of the darkness for only a fraction of a second before disappearing again. When I was finished I called to Sharon to shine her light down the tunnel so I could find my way out. I followed the feeble light out to the entrance. We left the building and came out blinking and squinting into the bright sunshine.

There are strange things going on at Widow McCleary's Pub. Whether the poor spirits of the McClearys cause them or the spirits served at the bar is anyone's guess.

Central

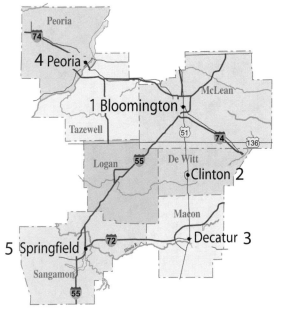

1 **Bloomington** (MCLEAN COUNTY)
      Pumpernickel's Deli & Eatery

2 **Clinton** (DEWITT COUNTY)
      C. H. Moore Homestead

3 **Decatur** (MACON COUNTY)
      Greenwood Cemetery

4 **Peoria** (PEORIA COUNTY)
      Meyer Jacobs Theatre, Bradley University
      Peoria Public Library
      Dana-Thomas House

5 **Springfield** (SANGAMON COUNTY)
      Inn at 835
      Abraham Lincoln Home
      Abraham Lincoln Tomb
      Vachel Lindsay Home
      Old State Capitol

Pumpernickel's Deli & Eatery
BLOOMINGTON

TERRY GROFF, A CO-OWNER OF PUMPERNICKEL'S
Deli & Eatery on North Center Street, in Bloomington, doesn't believe
in ghosts. That's what he's always said, but eerie events in the newly
opened restaurant have got him scratching his beard and wondering
if perhaps spooks do exist.

Pumpernickel's is located in the old brick Crothers & Chew
Building, erected in 1856 and listed on the National Register of Historic
Places. All old buildings have their share of unexplainable noises, but
not all of them have disembodied voices like the voice Terry heard in
the basement in the summer of 2004.

"I don't like the basement. It gives me the creeps," Terry said, as we sat in the dining room of the restaurant beside a Christmas tree decked out in glowing lights. Terry was a young guy in his early twenties, beefy in that typical Midwestern way, and I thought he could probably take care of himself just fine in case of trouble. But he was afraid of the basement.

"I was down there in the dark when I heard a voice say, 'Hello,'" Terry continued. "I thought someone had gotten into the basement, maybe a homeless person, so I got out quick and got my neighbor. Together, we checked out the basement, but no one was down there."

Terry said the voice sounded like a little girl, but since there was nobody to be found in the basement, he passed off the incident as a product of his imagination. But since that time, Terry has heard the same voice again. One late night in August he heard the little girl while he was alone in the building doing some paperwork. Another time he heard children laughing, although there were no children in the restaurant. He even went out into the street, looking for the source of the laughter but to no avail.

Erin Armstrong, a night waitress at the restaurant, also heard the little ghost say, "Hi, there," while she was turning down the lights in the restaurant one evening in September. She asked the cook if she had heard anything, but the cook had not.

This was all too much for Terry and he decided to investigate the ghost for himself.

"I did some research on the building and found out that it used to house a doctor's office, pharmacy, and living quarters. Abraham Lincoln supposedly gave a speech here, and there was also a little girl who died in a fire at the age of six. The newspapers did not give her first name but identified her as the eldest daughter of E. K. Crothers, the doctor," Terry said.

According to Terry, the 1859 newspaper account said that the little girl had caught her dress on fire from the stove in the house, a not uncommon type of accidental death for females in the nineteenth century.

"But there was no mention of her first name or where she was buried, so all that is still a mystery," Terry said. He thinks the little girl may be related to Rachel Crothers, probably the most prolific and successful female dramatist of the early twentieth century, although he has not yet been able to prove his claim.

As Terry and I talked, he kept his eyes on the customers coming and going in the busy restaurant in case he was needed to help out. It was a cheerful and convivial place, especially decorated as it was for Christmas, and the dozen or so tables in the small dining room were crowded. It seemed to me exactly the kind of place that a lost and lonely little girl would find inviting.

Terry said that there had been a sandwich shop in the space now occupied by Pumpernickel's, but it seemed the ghost did not make her presence known there. Terry and his business partner took possession of the space in February 2004 and made some renovations before opening in May.

"That may explain your ghost," I said. I explained to Terry the theory held by some researchers that ghosts become particularly active when physical changes are made to their environment, when their homes and businesses are tampered with by the present owners. "It's like the ghosts become nervous, anxious, thinking that maybe there will be no place for them when the work is done, or maybe they're angry that changes are being made."

Terry admitted that the voices started up shortly after the remodeling, but had not been heard for a few months. "Maybe she's getting used to it," Terry said.

I also asked Terry if he had ever had any psychic experiences before, since it seems that some people are more disposed to hear and see ghosts than others, more sensitive, one could say. His first response was negative, but a moment later he recollected that his mother had told him that when he was a little boy he used to talk to ghosts. Not just any ghosts, but the two that apparently haunted his house. His mother thought one ghost was good and the other bad.

"The funny thing is that she didn't tell me this until after I told her what was going on at the restaurant," Terry said. "I couldn't remember doing what she said I did, but she assured me that it had happened."

"So maybe you are sensitive to ghosts," I said, "or at least sensitive to this little girl ghost."

Terry seemed to give that some thought but didn't have anything more to say.

At least one of Pumpernickel's customers may also be sensitive to the ghost. Not too long ago a female patron who was in the ladies' room heard a child giggling outside the room, but when she came out there was no child, nor had any children been in the restaurant at the time.

Terry plans on continuing his research, hoping to conclusively identify the little spirit that longs for conversation, although he remains skeptical of some people who have claimed to know all about her, such as the psychic who simply parroted back the information Terry gave him as though he were revealing some great paranormal secret. A little skepticism is healthy for a researcher and I have the feeling that in time, Terry's attitude will pay off; he will come to know all there is to know about his little ghost.

C. H. Moore Homestead

CLINTON

I ALMOST DROVE RIGHT PAST THE C. H. MOORE Homestead in Clinton. My wife, Mary, and I were headed to Decatur from Bloomington, and I was focused on what I wanted to see in Decatur. Mary saw the signs for the DeWitt County Historical Museum and suggested, rather strongly I thought, that we turn off the highway to visit it. I had never heard of the museum before, and it was not on my research list of haunted places, so I was not happy about what I thought would be a delay in the serious business of ghosthunting.

Sometimes I'm an idiot. The C. H. Moore Homestead ended up being a place that gave me the willies, and for that I was indebted to my wife's intuition and not my own.

The house itself is a Victorian mansion built by John and Minerva Moore Bishop in 1867. John Bishop had done quite well for himself in the grain and lumber business and his house reflected his financial success. But money could not compensate for the tragic loss of the Bishop's only child, Mary Elizabeth, who died when she was two. When tragedy struck again and Bishop's wife died in the early 1880s, he sold the house to his brother-in-law, Clifton H. Moore.

Moore was a prominent attorney and friend of Abraham Lincoln. He did much in 1860 to help Lincoln secure the presidential nomination. In 1887, Moore added the west wing to the structure, including the two-story library to house his collection of more than 7,000 books, many of them rare and valuable editions. Moore opened his private library to the citizens of Clinton. He died in 1901, at the age of eighty-three, leaving a vast estate to his heirs.

Larry Buss related this history to me; he's a smiling and congenial man who I thought looked something like John Denver. Larry lives in and manages the homestead, which also includes the DeWitt County Historical Museum in the basement, as well as the Barn and Carriage House, the Farm Museum, and Telephone Exhibit on the grounds of the estate. We were talking in the kitchen of the house. Actually, Larry was talking at length while I was simply listening, taking it all in. His knowledge of the house and its history was impressive. After a while, Larry went back to his office, and I explored the house on my own.

The house was decorated in traditional Victorian Christmas style, the wonderful nostalgic stuff of Christmas cards and Hallmark television specials. In such a warm and inviting atmosphere it was difficult to think of ghosts, and yet some people think that the holidays actually bring on more paranormal activity. The theory is that during the holidays, ghosts feel especially lonely for the families and lives they once had, and the families remaining behind feel the loss of their loved ones even more. With so much psychic energy coming from both sides, ghostly activity seems inevitable. Perhaps Charles

Dickens understood that when he included not one but three ghosts in *A Christmas Carol.*

In the dining room a round table was set for four people with a snowy white tablecloth, red glassware, fine china with a flower design, and a large floral centerpiece flanked by white tapers. A Christmas tree stood in the corner of the room draped in green and white garland and hung with silver snowflakes and green and white balls.

The parlor's Christmas decorations were even more elaborate. Red ribbons and evergreen boughs draped the large gilt mirror over the mantel and the pictures on the walls. They dripped from the bright brass chandelier hanging in the center of the room and curled around the andirons on the hearth. Stockings were hung from the mantel with care. Poinsettias sat on the hearth. Evergreen wreaths hung in the windows. An enormous Christmas tree stood in the room, covered all over with red flowers and streamers and white garland. As if the red Christmas decorations were not enough, the walls were papered in a red-and-white pattern and scarlet valances capped the sheer white curtains covering the long windows. All that was needed to make complete the ideal Victorian Christmas was the Bishop's child sitting on the rug before the fireplace, opening her gaily wrapped presents.

On the opposite side of the house, across the wide entryway, was the library built by C. H. Moore. While men may fantasize about many things, a male writer fantasizes about his own library, and this one was the ultimate fantasy. Exquisitely carved, glass-fronted bookcases stood to one side of the room containing collections of old books. A unique circular bookrack occupied an opposite corner near a framed portrait of C. H. Moore. A large oak table and two chairs rested upon a Persian carpet in the center of the room. As in the other rooms of the mansion, Christmas wreaths, bows, and ribbons were everywhere. The most striking feature of the library, however, was the large oblong opening in the ceiling. Looking up, I saw that a wrought-iron rail surrounded it. More bookcases were visible beyond the rail. I was looking into Moore's private library, accessible only through his bedroom on the second floor.

Still, I wasn't seeing any ghosts. When I spoke to Larry earlier, he had told me that a psychic investigator from Springfield had visited the homestead only a week or two before my visit and had asked permission to conduct an investigation at the house. Larry had granted permission and the investigation was to be carried out sometime after the holidays. I asked Larry why the investigator wanted to study the homestead; did he have a hunch that it was haunted? Larry didn't think so and said the investigator was interested simply because the house was so old and mostly in the same condition it had been in years before. But I wondered if the investigator hadn't felt or sensed something at the homestead when he visited, something that prompted him to ask for a full-blown investigation.

I went up to the second floor. Four bedrooms, each of them appointed in antique furniture, were arranged off the wide hall. The rooms were light and airy, not at all what you would expect in a haunted house.

Moore's bedroom was at the end of the hall, facing out to the front of the house. I turned to the open doorway and my heart froze. There, standing by the bed, was a man wearing an old-fashioned nightshirt. He stood before a window, looking out, and seemed oblivious to my presence. My first thought was that I was at long last witnessing a psychic impression, an image from the past that, for unexplainable reasons, plays itself over and over again, the figures in the impression unaware of the viewer's presence and unable to interact with the viewer in any way. A psychic newsreel. After a second or two, I realized my ghost was a mannequin.

I went back downstairs and stopped to see Larry in his office. I asked him about ghosts again and he admitted to hearing strange noises in the house, although he believed they weren't anything you wouldn't expect in a house almost 150 years old.

"But I wonder sometimes," Larry said. "Once I heard the door to the gift shop open and close and I thought someone wanted to tour the house, so I went over to the area and called out, 'Hello,' but when I got there, no one was there."

Was that evidence of a ghost? I wondered.

After talking with Larry, I went outside to the carriage barn. Inside there were several different types of nineteenth-century vehicles on display; a few styles of horse-drawn carriages, two sleighs, a general-store delivery wagon, and even an old-fashioned high-wheeler bicycle. Harnesses and other equestrian tack hung on the walls. Old lanterns were suspended from the rafters, alongside drying shocks of corn. As I had done in the mansion, I took a few pictures inside the barn to be used as visual prompts to help me write this chapter.

I received an eerie surprise after downloading the pictures into my computer. There, in a photo taken in the carriage house, a large bright-blue orb floated above the leather seat of one of the carriages while another brilliant white one hovered near the ceiling. But even more remarkable was what appeared to be the figure of a little girl standing beside the carriage. She had long dark hair and was wearing a white dress. The faint and transparent image was about three feet tall, the grain in the wallboards clearly visible through her.

Orbs in C. H. Moore's
Carriage House

I showed the photo to Debbie Lowery, president of the Springfield Ghost Hunter's Society. She compared it to photos taken by her group during an investigation they had made at the Moore homestead early in 2005. Sure enough, the same image appeared in one of their photos as well. It was Debbie's opinion that the image was caused simply by the fading and weathering of the wooden walls. Perhaps that is the case, but that still might not rule out some paranormal explanation for the image. We have only to think of the countless images of Jesus

Mysterious little girl image
on the wall of the Carriage House

or the Virgin Mary that have appeared over the years in windows, on the sides of buildings, and even on major appliances to help us suspend our disbelief in miraculous or paranormal origins.

Furthermore, my scientist wife reminds me that scientists prove their theories by being able to successfully replicate the experiment, the implication in this case being that the image did, in fact, show up in photos other than my own. Still, Mary is a scientist and remains more of a skeptic than me, the befuddled, prone-to-flights-of-fancy writer.

I'm not yet entirely convinced that the figure was that of a ghost, but what if it was? Could it have been the ghost of little Mary Elizabeth Bishop? What better time could she have chosen to materialize than at Christmas, with all its magical wonders and childlike innocence?

Greenwood Cemetery

DECATUR

IT SEEMS THAT GREENWOOD CEMETERY IN DECATUR
is one of the few places in Illinois that is not haunted by the ghost of
Abraham Lincoln, but that's okay. It has enough ghosts even without
his presence. It's history as a burial place began with local Native
Americans and continues to this day.

Only a few days after Thanksgiving, my wife, Mary, and I
were driving around the streets of downtown Decatur looking for
Greenwood Cemetery. By pure dumb luck we found ourselves on
Lincoln Park Drive at the southern end of the city. The road took us

down around the cemetery, located upon several hills, to a parking lot along the Sangamon River. I parked in the lot, and we got out of the car. Directly before us, a hundred yards or so away, was the cemetery. Old stones clung to grassy knolls and rested beneath barren trees. Here and there a few dead trees lay toppled and shattered by a recent storm. A chain-link fence surrounded the cemetery at the base of the hill, and I realized that we were at the rear of the cemetery. There was no entrance.

It is in this rear section of the cemetery, among the hills and dales, where people have spotted ghost lights, mysterious globes of light that float through the night. The lights have been reported for decades. Troy Taylor, noted Illinois psychic researcher and one-time Decatur resident, saw the lights himself and came up with a possible explanation for them. According to Taylor, a flooding Sangamon River rose up over the rear section of the cemetery in the late 1800s, washing away tombstones, uncovering graves and sweeping away corpses and caskets. Days later, battered caskets and mangled corpses were still being fished from the river and recovered along the riverbanks. The corpses were reburied on higher ground in the cemetery, but many of them, including a large number of Civil War veterans, were unidentifiable and were reburied beneath headstones that read simply "Unknown U.S. Soldier." Some bodies that were swept away in the flood were never recovered. It is said that the ghost lights are the spirits of these unfortunate lost ones still roaming the hills of Greenwood Cemetery, searching for their remains.

Mary and I walked past the water treatment plant beside the parking lot and onto a paved bike path that ran parallel to the river, which was swift-moving and swollen with winter storm runoff. A red-tailed hawk lifted off from a dead tree only a few feet before us and took to the sky. We angled closer to the fence, slogging over marshy ground, trying to find a way into the cemetery. We followed the fence and eventually found a tear in it that allowed us to squeeze through. We were finally inside the cemetery, although in an unkempt fringe area below the hilltop graves. We trudged up a steep hill on the other side and came out on the cemetery road along the area where the

Civil War veterans were buried. It was a difficult way to enter the cemetery. A few minutes later we spotted the stone pillars at the main entrance off Church Street. We could have driven our car right into the cemetery.

One of the most famous ghostly residents of Greenwood Cemetery is the Greenwood Bride, a young woman who had made plans to elope with her bootlegger boyfriend back in the 1930s. As the woman waited for her lover at the appointed place on the night they were to run off together, he was murdered while delivering one last shipment of bootlegged booze. His killers tossed his body into the river. When the body was recovered the next day, the woman went wild with grief. She slipped away from her parents' house that night. In the morning her body was found floating in the river wearing the dress she had chosen for her wedding. Although the young woman was laid to rest upon a hill in Greenwood Cemetery, it seems that her spirit does not rest at all. Over the years, many people have seen a woman in a glowing white dress drifting among the headstones. Her head is bent in sorrow and she carries a handkerchief or scarf with which she wipes away her tears as she searches eternally for her lost lover.

We didn't see the Greenwood Bride as we walked through the cemetery, but we continued our exploration, thinking there was always the chance we might meet up with her later, or perhaps one of the many other ghosts who roam Greenwood.

We walked among the graves in the Civil War section atop a windswept hill. The naked tree branches overhead clacked together in the wind. An American flag snapped from its flagpole. Below us the ground sloped away to the rear fence. I could see our car parked in the paved lot beyond the fence. The headstones in this section were government issue and arranged in soldierly ranks among the terraces and down the slope of the hill. They were the graves of troops mostly from Illinois, Ohio, and Indiana, but among them were the dozens of unknown soldiers. Walking among their headstones, I wondered if they were not the spirits that flitted along the hillsides as ghost lights.

Troy Taylor writes in *Haunted Illinois* that the Civil War section is the most haunted part of the cemetery. He says that prisoner-of-war trains frequently passed through Decatur during the war and that one of them contained many dead soldiers, victims of yellow fever. Since the train passed close by the cemetery, the bodies of the dead Confederates were taken off the train and buried in a mass grave in the cemetery. Taylor says that in the soldiers' haste to bury the diseased bodies, it is possible that they buried alive some of the men who only appeared dead. If that wouldn't make ghosts out of them, and angry ghosts at that, nothing would.

We made our way downhill, back to the cemetery road. Another road entered from our right and merged with the first. The Barrackman family plot was located in that grassy wedge, recognizable by three stone steps overgrown with moss and half-buried under drifts of dead leaves. The top step bore the family name. The steps led up to a little hill upon which the Barrackman graves stood lined up in a neat row. There were four large headstones, those of Christian and Hannah Barrackman, their son William, and his wife, Harrietta. All were born in the nineteenth century; William and his wife both died before 1920. There was nothing remarkable about the family plot except for the fact that a weeping, ghostly girl has often been seen on the steps leading up to the graves, the very steps upon which Mary was seated while I photographed the graves. Who is this second sorrowful ghost? No one seems to know and I couldn't find any clues to her identity.

After we explored the cemetery, Mary and I returned to the car the same way we had come, through the fence. A dumb way to go, Mary pointed out, since we now knew where the road entered the cemetery, but male ghosthunters never ask for directions. As we drove back to our hotel in Peoria we thought we had put Greenwood Cemetery and its ghosts far behind us, but we had not. We pulled into an empty shopping center and stopped at a discount store just as it was closing for the day. We needed to pick up a few odds and ends. Let me be truthful here. It wasn't really "odds and ends." We had been on the road for well over a week and hadn't had a chance to wash our clothes; what we needed was new underwear. Okay? Are you happy now? Our car was the only one in the parking lot, but when we came out of the store, another car was parked directly beside ours. A woman stood there, her arms folded across her chest.

"Is this your car?" she called out, as we drew closer.

I hesitated. After all, the car she was talking about was a 1987 Buick Skyhawk painted all over with ghosts, demons, and haunted houses, along with slogans such as "Ghosthunter" and "I brake for hauntings." Would you admit to ownership of such a vehicle in a dark parking lot, facing a stranger who may or may not be a lunatic?

"Yes, that's my car," I bravely said, noting that she was cradling a little dog in her arms. "Why?"

The woman grinned. "Wow!" she said. "I saw you drive by and I just had to find out what you were all about, so I followed you here and waited for you to come out."

Okay, that's creepy, I thought. Mary hung back a little and I didn't blame her. After all, the woman was armed with a small dog.

The woman said her name was Skye* and she identified herself as a paranormal investigator. I explained that I was in Illinois researching haunted locations for a book. Skye was disappointed to hear that I didn't perform the technical investigations that she favored, using tape recorders, electromagnetic meters, motion detectors, multiple cameras, and all the other electronic gear in vogue with her colleagues.

"So, you're not *really* a ghosthunter," she said, glancing at the logo on the door of the car that proclaimed I was.

Ouch, that hurt. "More like a ghostwriter," I admitted.

Despite my diminished stature in her eyes, Skye went on to suggest various places for Mary and me to visit, including Greenwood Cemetery. When I told her we had just returned from there, she told me about her own experiences in the cemetery.

Skye and a friend of hers snuck into Greenwood at night and witnessed balls of floating light. They also saw dark figures moving through the cemetery, one of which stood upon a hill and was surrounded by an orange glow. The figure raised her—Skye was sure it was female—hand high above her head and it "dripped fire."

"You know," Skye said, "like when you set fire to a plastic milk jug."

I had never done that so I took her word for it.

Skye also said that she met the cemetery caretaker, who told her that he had once come across a man wearing an old military uniform. The soldier seemed confused and asked the caretaker where he was before disappearing like smoke.

"The caretaker says he never goes into the cemetery at night anymore," Skye said.

We talked for a few more minutes before I was finally able to politely break off the conversation and get into the car. "Well, that was interesting," I said to Mary as we drove away.

"Yes, it was," Mary said. "Cute dog, though."

Meyer Jacobs Theatre, Bradley University

PEORIA

I DON'T USUALLY WRITE ABOUT HAUNTED COLLEGES and universities because so many of the hauntings occur in dormitories that are not accessible to the general public, and I like my readers to be able to visit the locations in my books. But when my friend Kevin Stein, who teaches at Bradley University and is also the State of Illinois' Poet Laureate said he had heard tales of the university's theatre being haunted, I was intrigued. Anyone can visit a theatre—why not a haunted theatre?

Kevin referred me to Jim Langley, an associate professor in the university's Department of Theatre Arts. I met Jim in his office at the Hartmann Center for the Performing Arts, an attractive white stone building with a steeply pitched roof and large windows that gave the edifice the appearance of a Dutch burgher's home in old Amsterdam. Inside was the Meyer Jacobs Theatre and on the floors above, faculty offices. Jim's office was on the second floor.

I had been in central Illinois for almost two weeks researching various haunted sites and everywhere I went, no matter what story I was researching, there was always another tale about Abraham Lincoln. Town after town, story after story. He's even on Illinois license plates: The Land of Lincoln. So I wasn't surprised when Abraham Lincoln greeted me in Jim's office. He wore jeans and hiking boots, a dark-brown suede vest over a denim shirt. Full beard, and longish hair curling over his shirt collar. But it turned out that this wasn't Lincoln after all. Lincoln was only six foot four; this guy stood six seven. I guess they grow them tall in Illinois— something in the water maybe—and even though Jim Langley was not originally from Illinois, he must have been drinking that water.

Jim was very friendly and never once gave me the stink-eye because I was asking him about ghosts. In fact, he had had his own encounter with the Lady in Brown, as the theatre ghost is called, and so he kept an open mind about such things. Jim recalled that night, ten or eleven years ago, when he was working in the theatre alone, painting some "flats," stage sets. The flat was a piece of muslin ten feet square stretched over a wooden frame.

"It was late at night. The flat I was working on was laying on the stage directly over the trap door that goes down into the storage area below the stage and leads to the orchestra pit," Jim said.

After painting the set, Jim went to clean his brushes.

"When I came back, I saw three footprints in the wet paint, right in the middle of the set," he said. Jim described the footprints as being those of a lady's old-fashioned boot, with a small heel and pointed toe. "If it was a hoax of some kind, I can't figure out how anyone could have stepped into the middle of that flat without breaking it or making other prints."

"That was quite awhile ago," I said. "No one has come forward to admit the trick?"

Jim looked out the large bay window of his office. In the distance the university clock tower rose above the trees. Students hurried to class on the sidewalks below, their breath frosty in the cold November air. After a few moments he turned back to me.

"I didn't believe in ghosts before I came here," he said, "but now, let's just say I'm more open to the idea. And in answer to your question, no, no one ever admitted they pulled a trick on me. Sort of defeats the purpose of such an elaborate trick in the first place, doesn't it?"

"I would think so," I said.

Jim went on to say that although he did not have any other encounters with the ghost, several students had seen her over the years, especially standing in the dark tunnel below the stage that leads to the orchestra pit.

"Do you know who the ghost is?"

"We don't have a real name for her," Jim said, "but it's believed that she was a student in the music department back in the thirties. This building was originally built as a gymnasium and was called Hewitt Hall. It's said that the student drowned in the swimming pool that used to be here, directly below the stage. Would you like to see it?"

Would I? What a question to ask a ghosthunter!

I followed Jim downstairs to the theatre. We went inside and walked out onto the stage. He moved aside a rolling cart loaded with what I assumed were stage sets, revealing a trap door in the stage.

"This is awkward to handle," he said. "Do you mind giving me a hand?"

We squatted on opposite sides of the door, grabbed hold of the ringbolts, lifted up the door and slid it aside. I was looking down into a black hole with an iron ladder bolted to one side.

Jim sat on the edge of the hole, swung his legs over to the ladder and nimbly dropped down out of sight. Here goes nothing, I thought, and followed him down, although with considerably less grace.

"Sorry, there are no lights down here," Jim said.

We were standing at the bottom of the shaft and some light from the stage made its way down there, enough that I could see a wall to my left disappearing into the darkness beyond. The wall was painted pale blue.

"That's the original wall of the pool," Jim said, "so the stage now sits right over the old pool area."

"What's ahead?" I said, indicating the blackness before me.

"It's a tunnel that we use for storage. At the end, it turns left and enters the orchestra pit, which is covered now. During a performance we uncover it for the orchestra."

"And the Lady in Brown is seen in this hall?"

"Yes, she seems partial to musicals and likes to be near the music," Jim said.

I started down the hall, slowly since I couldn't see where I was going. There was enough headroom for my five-foot-eight-inch frame, but not for poor Jim, so he hung back.

"Careful where you step," he called, "there's a lot of junk down here."

It was quiet beneath the stage, like being in a cave, and dusty. I could feel my nose twitching. I had my camera with me and, remembering its powerful flash, I pointed it straight ahead and depressed the shutter. The hall exploded into light and in that second I saw a pile of boards stacked up against a black concrete block wall, exposed rafters overhead, a concrete floor layered in dust, but no ghost.

I made my way back out of the tunnel, following behind Jim. We pulled ourselves up the ladder and replaced the trap door, restoring the Lady in Brown's privacy.

"Some students have also seen her on one of the catwalks," Jim said, leading me over to a set of stairs that took us above the stage.

I may not be afraid of ghosts, but heights? Oh, yeah. I wear a parachute when I have to use a kitchen stepstool.

I stayed close to the wall as we made our way along the row of lights hanging down over the stage and was envious of Jim's nonchalance at such heights. Sure, easy for him, I thought. He's a lot taller than me; he didn't have as far to fall.

Jim walked to the end of the catwalk and showed me where the ghost likes to stand to watch a performance. "Of course, it's always pretty dark up here, a lot of shadows, easy to see things, I suppose. Still, there have been students who have been reluctant to come up here and who would swear they saw the ghost."

Back downstairs Jim told me about a second presence in the theatre, an unknown force that seems to be responsible for messing around with the electricity, causing disturbances with the lights and sound equipment. The "wumpus," as the students call it, had been active for some time in the theatre, much to the annoyance of those working on stage, until one student inadvertently trapped the wumpus. He was building a crash box—a wooden cube that is filled with loose junk metal, sealed, then rolled across the stage to produce sound effects—when he heard the pieces of metal clanking around on their own while the box was not moving. The student quickly nailed the lid on the box and that was the end of the theatre's electrical problems. At least for a little while. About eight years later, someone unsealed the lid of the crash box in order to rebuild it. The problems started up all over again.

Whether it's the Lady in Brown, a wumpus, or both, some strange things are happening at Bradley University's Meyer Jacobs Theatre. They wouldn't surprise Shakespeare, whose Hamlet says, "Horatio, there are more things in heaven and earth than are dreamt of in your philosophy."

Peoria Public Library

PEORIA

I DON'T KNOW WHY IT IS GHOSTS LIKE TO HAUNT
libraries, unless it's because they want to be the first to check out the
latest Stephen King novel. Whatever the attraction, it was working big
time at the Peoria Public Library.

In October I had called Trisha Noak, the library's public relations
coordinator, from my home in Ohio to find out about scheduling an
author's appearance at the library. To my surprise, Trisha thought I
was calling her to hear about the library's own ghost stories! This is
the way I find my stories sometimes; it's almost as though the spirits

conspire to assist me. Two months later, I was pulling into the parking lot beside the concrete and steel block that was the Peoria Public Library in downtown Peoria.

Although the library's exterior is nondescript, it holds some real treasures within. The first of these treasures that Trisha showed me after greeting me at the main desk was a huge church antiphony kept securely in a glass case in the main lobby. The book dated from 1500 and had once belonged to a German order of Poor Claires. The plainsong music notes looked as fresh as if they had been written that day. A second display case held a collection of Davy Crockett memorabilia from the 1950s. The kids' coonskin cap and lunchbox took me back to my youth. Davy Crockett and German plainsong, such a weird juxtaposition, I thought. No wonder the ghosts liked this place.

And where were those ghosts?

Trisha told me that several people had died at the library. One was a man who waited in the library's vestibule for his court appearance at the courthouse across the street. Apparently, he knew his case was hopeless. He swallowed cyanide and dropped dead right where he stood. One of the library's directors, Dr. Edwin Wiley, killed himself in 1924 by ingesting arsenic. He was only fifty-two when he died and one of several library directors to die before reaching the age of sixty.

"Some people say there is a curse at work," said Trisha.

"How so?" I asked.

"Three in a row," Trisha said, as she told me about some of the past directors. There was E. S. Wilcox, who was struck and killed by a streetcar in 1915 as he stepped into the street before the library. He was followed by S. Patterson Prowse, who was felled by a heart attack during an argument at a board meeting in the library in 1921. He was succeeded by Wiley, who it turns out, had tried to kill himself at least twice before and had once been confined to a mental asylum.

We were riding in the elevator while Trisha told me these stories. Just as we stepped off, she said, "Wait. Stand right there," and indicated a place by the elevator door.

I stood on the spot she had pointed out.

"What do you feel?" she asked.

I stood there for a moment, unaware of any different feelings. Then it hit me. First, a cold spot. Then I felt as though I were floating, as if my feet had lifted off the floor. At the same time, I suddenly felt lightheaded, slightly dizzy.

"Wow!" was all I could say.

Trisha smiled and nodded her head. "Weird, isn't it? Everybody feels that, but we don't know what causes it."

I stepped to one side and the odd sensations vanished. I wondered if somehow the elevator's movement was the cause, but it had not been moving when I stood on the spot. It was weird, all right, but was it evidence of ghosts?

As if she had heard my silent musing, Trisha led me into a small office that held two desks and some filing cabinets. She introduced me to Rita, who was enjoying a lunch break at one of the desks.

"This is where I had my own encounter with a ghost," said Trisha.

She explained that she and Rita had been working together in the office. She said that Rita got up from her desk and walked toward the wall. As she walked, the lights above her flickered. Trisha saw Rita's chair suddenly "shoot across the floor" a distance of about three feet. Rita had her back turned to the chair and didn't see it move, but she wasn't surprised that it had happened. She told me that she often hears strange sounds in the office, coming from the wall.

"It sounds like wailing, like someone's in pain," Rita said.

There were more ghost stories from the library, but Trisha wanted me to hear them from the people who had experienced them, so we continued on our tour. We made a brief visit to the director's office, where I met the current library director, Bob Black. He told me he was almost sixty and, while aware of the lousy luck of former directors, he hoped to outlive his predecessors. He was a nice guy; I wished him the best of luck.

In the children's literature section we met up with Elizabeth*, a custodian who had worked at the library for several years. She was a diminutive woman, shy but friendly. At first, she was hesitant to talk about her experiences, but with just a little gentle prodding from Trisha, she opened up.

She told us about the time she had seen an elderly, well-dressed man in black wandering around in the library. She got up from where she had been sitting to see if she could assist him, when he disappeared without a trace.

"I know who it was, though. He looked just like Wilcox," Elizabeth said, referring to the director who had been squashed flat by the streetcar.

That wasn't all Elizabeth had seen. She said that a book fell off a shelf all by itself as she was cleaning in the room. She went to it, picked it up, and put it back on the shelf. A moment later, it popped off the shelf again.

"I just told them to stop it," Elizabeth said. "I didn't have time for nonsense, and when I said that, two books fell off the shelf."

But that was nothing, she said. Elizabeth told us that another custodian, Richard Partee, had been waxing the floor when books started falling from a shelf one by one. When the first shelf emptied, the books on the next shelf started falling out.

Elizabeth is sure there is something or several unexplainable somethings in the library. She said that she even ran into one of them with her cleaning cart. Something had dropped from her cart and she bent down to pick it up. As she did, she accidentally pushed the cart forward and it bumped into what she thought was a person. She apologized to the person, but when she looked up, there was no one there.

On another occasion she and Richard were in the library basement with the man who serviced the vending machines. He was a student of the paranormal and had read a story about the library's supposed curse. He asked the two custodians to take him down to the basement. He had barely arrived there, Elizabeth said, when he looked down the rows of dimly lit book stacks and saw ghosts. The man said that they were running away, hiding from the human intruders.

More often than not, it seems that the ghostly phenomena going on at the library occur in the early hours, as the library is opening, or late at night, when few staffers are around.

Stacy, a library staffer, was alone in the building one night, closing up. She was filling a coffee pot in a sink located near the doors to the auditorium. As the pot filled, she heard a metallic clicking sound as though someone were working the locked doors of the auditorium, trying to get through. Stacy checked the doors, but there was no one there. She didn't waste any time in leaving the building.

Cynthia, another library staffer, also had a run-in with a ghostly visitor when she was alone in the basement stacks. Something flicked her ears from behind, knocking off her earrings and sending them flying about fifteen feet. She was momentarily startled as anyone would be, but not particularly afraid, an interesting reaction I have noticed in many haunted locations. Immediate surprise, followed by curiosity, but an experience so often devoid of Hollywood-style terror.

"It really didn't bother me at all," Cynthia said. "I'm more afraid of the living than I am of the dead."

Trisha and the others know there is something strange going on at the library, but a thorough investigation has not yet been made. Perhaps someday there will be real documentation of the library's ghosts. In the meantime, it is comforting to know that those old directors of the past are still watching over the library.

Dana-Thomas House
SPRINGFIELD

THERE ARE TWO GOOD REASONS TO VISIT THE DANA-
Thomas House at 301 East Lawrence Avenue in Springfield. The first
is that the house is the most complete and best preserved of Frank
Lloyd Wright's early "Prairie-style" houses. The second reason is that
you just might bump into the ghost of Susan Lawrence Dana, who
had the house constructed in 1904.

It was an overcast winter's day when I visited the Dana-Thomas
house; Wright's ribbon art glass windows were dull and lackluster
in the flat light. Dried and withered vines hung lifelessly over the
stone walls. Icy water dripped from the wide overhanging eaves of

the low-rise roof. Faint lights were only dimly visible behind the dark windows, and I wasn't sure whether the house was open. I found the main entrance on the Lawrence Avenue side of the house, an unpretentious single door set beneath a brick arch, but I was politely shooed away from there by a volunteer who directed me to the rear of the building, where public tours originated in what used to be the old carriage house.

There was a tour about to begin in just a few minutes, so I waited in the narrow reception hall with a dozen or so other people. After a while we were admitted into a nondescript room and shown a movie about the house. When the lights came up, our tour guide, a corpulent elderly man in suspenders who used a cane to support him, led us into the house proper.

Although the Dana-Thomas house was electrified, the wattage was low—little more than candlelight—as it would have been in the early twentieth century, which meant that the interior of the house was dim and gloomy. If it were not for Frank Lloyd Wright's modern open floor plan with rooms flowing into one another, it would have been dark indeed.

Susan Lawrence Dana's original idea for her new house was to somehow incorporate the thirty-year-old brick Italianate house originally built on the property by her wealthy father, Rheuna Lawrence, into the floor plan of the new house. As Wright developed his designs, however, the old house was completely swallowed up by the new. The only concession to the original house was a small Victorian-style sitting room with a marble fireplace. The rest of the house was avant-garde for its day.

Our guide led us into the atrium, decorated with furniture and artwork all designed by Wright. Above us, a gallery ran along three sides of the open room. As I stood there looking up, I felt as though I were standing in a medieval palazzo eagerly awaiting the appearance on the balcony of some member of the nobility. But the gallery was dimly lit and, if anything walked through its shadows, I never saw it.

The house clearly bore the stamp of Susan Lawrence Dana's modernism and her progressive thought, but it also preserved the memories of a life beset by tragedy. Susan was the only surviving child of Rheuna and Mary Agnes Maxcy Lawrence and grew up in an elegant and lavish lifestyle. In 1883 she married Edwin Dana, a young real estate entrepreneur. The couple lived for a few years in St. Paul, Minnesota, where Susan bore two children, both of whom died in infancy. In the 1890s the Danas moved back to Springfield. Edwin was killed in Oregon in 1900 while inspecting a mine owned by his father-in-law. Only a few months later, Susan's father died.

Upon her father's death, Susan became executor of his estate. She and her mother hired Wright to build the new house and dedicated it with a series of elaborate Christmas parties. Susan's mother died just months after the house was completed. In 1912, Susan married a young Danish baritone concert artist named Lawrence Joergen-Dahl, who died unexpectedly the following year. Her third marriage to Charles Gehrmann ended in divorce.

Dana entertained often and with great social distinction, hosting not only benefit concerts for charitable causes, but politicians, members of society, and international celebrities as well. Our group made its way into the dining room with its barrel-vaulted ceiling. A long table, covered with a snowy white cloth and glittering place settings for thirty people, took up most of the space. Huge floral displays were placed strategically upon it. I could almost hear the animated chatter of Susan's guests and the tinkling of glasses and silverware in the silent house.

Later in life, Susan developed a strong interest in metaphysical matters and mystical religious groups. She hosted gatherings of members of the Unity and Baha'i churches and even founded her own group, the Lawrence Center for Constructive Thought, which often gathered at the house to discuss things metaphysical. It is thought that Susan was also enamored of spiritualism and held séances in the house to obtain advice, especially regarding financial issues, from her deceased father.

In 1928, Susan's cousin Flora, who had lived in the house with Susan for many years, died. Susan's own deteriorating health, as well as her growing financial difficulties—apparently, the séances were of little help—caused her to move out of the house into smaller quarters. She was ultimately placed in a hospital and declared incompetent. The house, now in bad repair, was managed by a conservator and many of its fine furnishings and art pieces were sold off at a fraction of their true worth. Charles C. Thomas, a book publisher and admirer of Frank Lloyd Wright, saved the house from oblivion. Thomas repaired the house and moved his publishing company into it. Later, it was purchased by the State of Illinois and restored to its 1910 condition. Many of its original furnishings were recovered and returned to the house.

Although the house doesn't look very tall from the outside, it actually has sixteen different levels inside. Our guide led us to the gallery above the atrium and through the various rooms. One of them was the bedroom Susan shared with her cousin Flora. Despite Susan's immense wealth, the bedroom, while large, was simple in decoration and furnished sparsely. Susan's bed was small and unpretentious. A single pillow lay upon it and our guide informed us that Susan always slept with a pistol and knife beneath her pillow. Many years after it had been sold, the pistol was recovered and once again placed beneath her pillow, should Susan's spirit ever have need of it.

As for her spirit, it was nowhere in evidence the day I visited. It was not in the bedroom, or the lavish dining room, or even the huge upstairs ballroom, where a fourteen-foot-tall Christmas tree stood, decked out in its holiday finery. So, what made the Dana-Thomas House haunted? Was it simply its connection to Spiritualism? Considering the fact that Spiritualists routinely communicate with ghosts, it was not at all far-fetched to think that some of those spirits might still be lingering in the gloom of the house. I asked our tour guide if there were ghosts in the house, but he suddenly went deaf and didn't give me an answer. There are two answers to that question that always make me suspicious. One is the too quick, unequivocal "no." The other is silence.

Illinois psychic researcher Troy Taylor has reported on some strange goings-on in the house. He mentions in *Haunted Illinois* that the site superintendent, Don Hallmark, once heard a human hand clap late one night while only he and his wife were in the house. They were in the downstairs corridor that contains a bowling alley, locking up the house for the night, when he heard the sound that nearly made him "jump out of his skin." Hallmark's wife also heard the sound. Despite all their efforts to come up with a plausible explanation for the sound, they were unable to do so.

A few years after that incident, on the thirty-seventh anniversary of Susan Lawrence Dana's death, a light sconce suddenly broke free of the wall and fell to the floor. Don Hallmark said at the time that unless someone had tampered with it—and he was sure no one had—there was no way the sconce could have fallen.

One certainly must wonder about such incidents happening in a house that is not supposed to be haunted, especially in light of Susan's interest in Spiritualism. Perhaps some investigative group will conduct a thorough study of the Dana-Thomas House and meet the spirit of Susan Lawrence Dana face to face.

Inn at 835

SPRINGFIELD

"I'VE LIVED HERE TEN YEARS AND I'VE NEVER HAD any experiences with ghosts," said Court Conn, who, along with his wife, Karen, owns and operates the Inn at 835 on South Second Street in downtown Springfield. Court stood by the fireplace, leaning his wiry frame against the mantel. A cheery fire crackled in the grate. A large Christmas tree, glowing with lights, stood in the corner. My wife, Mary, and I sat in comfortable wing chairs by the fire, sipping zinfandel. "But maybe I'm just not in tune with them," he added, thoughtfully.

The lighting in the parlor where we talked was low, similar to how it would have been in 1909 when Springfield entrepreneur Bell Miller built the six-flat apartment building that the Conns converted into a bed and breakfast in 1997. It was easy to imagine ghosts in the shadows just beyond the lamplight's glow and there was something about the graceful elegance of the building that made me think any resident ghosts were there simply because they enjoyed the place too much to move on. So much better than a run-down abandoned farmhouse or drafty old castle, I thought.

Bell Miller was ahead of her time when she built the apartment building, one of the first in Springfield. She had already been a successful businesswoman in a time when very few women were in business. Her floral enterprise began in modest quarters but soon expanded to several large greenhouses sprawled in the neighborhood where she built the building. The six flats were luxurious by the standards of her day and included servants' quarters and private verandahs for warm summer days. The lobby and stairs were all done in quarter sawn carved oak, and rich hardwood floors flowed from room to room.

In restoring the building, the Conns kept Bell's original vision alive, and perhaps that is why ghosts still linger there.

Mary and I were checked into the Poppy Room, number 204, on the second floor. It featured a queen-sized canopy bed, ceiling fan, Jacuzzi bath, antique dresser and writing desk, two comfortable side chairs, and—always important to a writer on the go—a DSL connection for my computer. A door led out to the verandah, although the snow that dusted the wicker chairs did not make it very inviting. Still, we thought the Poppy Room was comfortable, which is why I was surprised when Sally Hays told me it was one of the rooms that was reported to be haunted. Of course, we hadn't yet spent the night there.

We had just come back to the inn from dinner in town. Mary, braver than I would have been, went upstairs alone to the room while I stayed to talk with Sally, the night innkeeper. Sally sat behind the counter. She was a middle-aged blonde with shoulder-length hair who said she had worked at the inn for only a year. With the exception of a single lamp on the front desk counter, the small lobby was dark. The wood trim glowed warmly where the light reached it but shadows gathered above and around us. I felt like we were in a scene from *The Shining*.

In the year that Sally worked the night desk, sometimes being the only person in the entire building, she had experienced enough strange things to make her think the inn was haunted.

"There was a book placed squarely on the table in the room just around the corner," she said, gesturing to a room off to her right. "I was alone that night and I saw the book as I passed by. I came back behind the desk and a little later heard something fall to the floor in that room. I went back to look and there was the book lying on the floor. There's no way it could have flown off the table by itself."

Sally said that she also felt cold spots throughout the building and sometimes detected a strong floral fragrance, what she called the "scent of funeral flowers." She has also heard doors closing and the floorboards creaking, all sounds you might expect to hear in a building almost one hundred years old, but sounds you don't want to hear when you are alone in the building.

One of those sounds was a woman's voice heard by Don Bailey, who lived in one of the apartments from 1992 to 1997, just before the building's conversion into an inn. According to a story published in one of the local papers, Bailey was alone in his apartment when he heard a warm and pleasant woman's voice say, "Well, hello there!" Bailey thought that his wife had come home with a friend—the voice did not sound like his wife's—but after checking the apartment, he found himself alone. Bailey heard the same voice only a few weeks later as he was decorating the apartment for Christmas.

"Well, I see we're getting ready for the holidays!" the voice said.

Bailey thought his wife, Velma, who was in the kitchen at the opposite end of the apartment, had spoken to him. She said she had not. He never heard the voice again.

As we talked at the front desk, Sally told me that there were three rooms in the inn that had strange experiences associated with them, the Orchid Suite, Room 304, and the Poppy Room, occupied by Mary and me.

"What makes those rooms haunted?" I asked, thinking it might be better if I had some warning of what I might expect later.

"They're all different," Sally said. "The Orchid Suite is probably the worst."

She told me about a bride-to-be who was staying there with some members of her bridal party. The bride just could not shake the feeling that someone was watching her, and she kept the lights on in the suite all through the night. The next day she checked out and went to a different hotel.

There was also Angie and Tracey Sidles, a young couple who were in the Orchid Suite celebrating their first wedding anniversary. Angie tried to take a Jacuzzi bath but couldn't get the jets to work properly and gave up. A few minutes later, while the couple was "watching television," they heard the shower suddenly come on. The shower could only be turned on by first pulling up a lever that would block the flow of water to the bathtub. How in the world could that lever have pulled itself up? Tracey checked out the shower and found that the jets in the Jacuzzi were also shooting up water. He came back into the bedroom and began throwing their clothes in a suitcase, despite Angie's desire to stay and see what else would happen.

Sally laughed when she told me that story. "Ghost or no ghost," she said, "I didn't think it was necessary for them to check out."

The Sidles apparently thought otherwise as they departed the inn in the middle of the night.

"What about my room?" I asked.

"I can't explain it," Sally said. "I just find it unwelcoming, really creepy. I can't stand to go into it."

That didn't sound like I had much to fear, although I had to remember that Sally was probably more in tune with the spirits of the house than I was. It seemed that the Conns' dogs were also in tune with them. Court had told Mary and me earlier that their two pugs would sometimes stare into space as though watching something unseen to human eyes. Of course, we were talking about pugs, a breed of dog whose eyes sometimes fall out of its head—I swear that's true—so who knows what they were really seeing, if anything at all.

Sally also told me that she sometimes saw things "float by" as she worked at the night desk. She never saw these things straight on, but always from her peripheral vision. As mentioned earlier in the book, there is a theory that may explain these "corner ghosts," as they are called, ghosts seen from the "corners" of our eyes. Some researchers believe that ghosts exist in the infrared light zone, a part of the spectrum the human eye cannot usually detect, although a thin ring around the iris allows us to see partly into the infrared at times, and from the periphery of our field of vision. That's when we catch our corner ghosts, if only fleetingly.

I thought about Sally's corner ghosts later that night. Mary was happily bubbling away in the Jacuzzi while I was reading in our room. Suddenly, I saw something move from the corner of my eye. I stopped reading and turned. Nothing. I went back to my reading and only a few minutes later, it happened again, this time slightly above me. When I looked up, nothing. I didn't feel afraid, only distracted and annoyed as one might be if harried by a persistent horsefly. I returned to my book and for a third time, I detected something move, this time from my right. I finally gave in and closed my book and, of course, I was not bothered again.

To be honest, I don't know if I had truly experienced corner ghosts or not. My eyesight is terrible, on a scale somewhere between pop-eyed pugs and cavefish, so my experiences may not prove that corner ghosts visited me. Perhaps some steely-eyed person with perfect 20-20 vision would make a better test subject.

The rest of the night was uneventful, although not entirely restful. I woke up several times throughout the night, unusual for me, who would sleep through the trumpets announcing the Second Coming if they sounded after dark. Mary was awake as well. It wasn't as though we were startled awake by anything, we simply found ourselves peering into the dark wondering why we were awake. Repeatedly. This had happened to us once before, when we stayed at a haunted inn in Ohio as I was researching my first ghost book, *Ghosthunting Ohio*, but then we had also felt some uneasiness in the room and had heard some unusual sounds. That was not the case at the Inn at 835. We simply kept waking up for no apparent reason.

It could just be that the ghosts at the Inn at 835 are a more considerate lot than those at the Ohio inn. Wake you up, yes, but quietly, calmly. No theatrics. That's really not so bad, is it?

Abraham Lincoln Home

SPRINGFIELD

WHEN SELF-TAUGHT LAWYER ABRAHAM LINCOLN
rode his horse into Springfield in 1837, all his meager belongings were
packed into two saddlebags. Five years later the rising young attorney
married Mary Todd, a well-educated woman from a prominent
Kentucky family, and in 1844 the Lincolns paid $1,500 for a Greek-
Revival cottage at the corner of Eighth and Jackson Streets. For the
next seventeen years the house—considerably enlarged by Lincoln—
sheltered the growing family. Three of his four children were born

there and one of them, Edward, died in the house at the age of four.

On February 11, 1861, the Lincolns left Springfield by train, headed for Washington, DC, where Lincoln would be sworn in as the sixteenth president of the United States. He never again saw his Springfield home, but in 1865 his somber funeral cortege passed before the house, decked out in black and white bunting, as it made its way to Oak Ridge Cemetery, where the murdered president was laid to rest.

Since then, some visitors to the Lincoln home have reported seeing a tall, thin apparition with a little boy, perhaps Abe and little Edward. Most visitors who experience a paranormal event in the house, however, say that it is the ghost of Mary Todd Lincoln who lingers there, in the place where she lived the happiest years of her adult life. That may be, although none of the National Park Service rangers I met at the Lincoln Home would admit the presence of any ghosts. They couldn't fool me, however. I knew why they couldn't talk about the ghosts; according to the USA PATRIOT Act, any admission on their part that ghosts haunted the national landmark would jeopardize national security.

Even so, I ventured on a tour of the house to see for myself if it was haunted.

Abraham Lincoln was no stranger to events that some might call supernatural. He once related such an event to a few friends, one of them being Noah Brooks. After Lincoln's assassination, Brooks told the story to the readers of *Harper's New Monthly Magazine*, recounting the story "as nearly as possible in his own words":

"It was just after my election in 1860. . . I was well tired out, and went home to rest, throwing myself down on a lounge in my chamber. Opposite where I lay was a bureau, with a swinging-glass upon it—[and here he got up and placed furniture to illustrate the position]—and, looking in that glass, I saw myself reflected, nearly at full length; but my face, I noticed, had two separate and distinct images, the tip of the nose of one being about three inches from the tip of the other. I was a little bothered, perhaps startled, and got up and looked in the glass, but the illusion vanished. On lying down again I saw it a second time—plainer, if possible, than before; and then I noticed that one of the faces was a little paler, say five shades, than the other. I got up and the thing melted away, and I went off and, in the excitement of the hour, forgot all about it—nearly, but not quite, for the thing would once in a while come up, and give me a little pang, as though something uncomfortable had happened. When I went home I told my wife about it, and a few days after I tried the experiment again, when [with a laugh], sure enough, the thing came again; but I never succeeded in bringing the ghost back after that, though I once tried very industriously to show it to my wife, who was worried about it somewhat. She thought it was 'a sign' that I was to be elected to a second term of office, and that the paleness of one of the faces was an omen that I should not see life through the last term."

Ward Hill Lamon, another close friend of Lincoln's had also been told the story, but it was his impression that Lincoln shared his wife's belief that the double image meant death for him.

That mirror is not in the Springfield house and is lost to history, as are many of the personal items owned by the Lincolns during that time. Lincoln sold most of his furniture when he moved to Washington and a good portion of it ended up with owners in Chicago, where it was destroyed in the 1871 fire that almost obliterated that city. The horsehair-covered side chairs and couch in the parlor did belong to the Lincolns, however, and the latter may be the "lounge" Lincoln mentioned to Brooks.

The parlor floor was carpeted in burgundy with a busy green-and-white floral pattern running through it. Wallpaper of silver vines, bearing coppery flowers, covered the walls. Red and gold curtains hung at the windows. The overall effect was something like a bad hangover, but was typical of nineteenth-century design.

One of the furniture parlor pieces actually owned by the Lincolns was the horsehair rocker that sat to one side of the hearth, the same rocker that had been seen by several people over the years to set itself rocking without anyone touching it. Or maybe someone does rock it, perhaps Mrs. Lincoln, since some visitors to the house have seen her unmistakable figure standing in the parlor for an instant before vanishing, while others have heard the rustling of her skirts passing them in the hall.

The park ranger escorted our tour group through the Lincoln home rather brusquely, even though there were not many visitors that day, so I didn't get the chance to just sit quietly awhile and meditate, a practice I like to do at historic sites. In many ways that simple practice puts me more in tune with the place, its history, and those who have gone before. If there is any psychic history attached to the place, I believe this is one way to connect with it.

But we were already on the second floor of the house, an addition Lincoln added to the original cottage to accommodate his growing family. A small round shaving mirror in a fanciful wood frame hung on the wall at an impossible height above a ceramic pitcher and basin sitting on a washstand. The six-foot-four-inch future president used the mirror to shave his face—he didn't grow his beard until he came to Washington—but when I looked in it, all I could see was the top of my head. Although the mirror had been an item actually owned by the Lincolns, it was too small to be the mirror in which he saw the twin reflections.

We whisked through the remaining rooms and, try as I might, I simply could not get a sense of Lincoln the man. A few minutes later I was standing on the boardwalk outside the home asking other rangers about the ghosts. No one wanted to talk about them and I wondered if perhaps my Ghostmobile, an old 1987 Buick Skyhawk completely painted over with ghosts and demons and parked in the visitors center parking lot, had tipped them off. Maybe I had ratcheted up the security alert a color shade or two, who knows?

The park employees may have been reticent that day, but at least one of them had spoken out about the ghosts in the past. Shirlie Laughlin, an employee at the Abraham Lincoln Home, told of her experiences there in a 1998 interview with a reporter from Arlington

Heights's *Daily Herald*:

"I was rearranging the furniture in Mary Todd Lincoln's bedroom not long ago, trying to decide whether to move a small chair into another room. Something—someone—kept touching me on the shoulder. I kept looking around, but no one was there. I left that chair right where it was."

Shirlie also reported seeing the rocker in the parlor move and said that she could feel "wind rushing down the hall" despite the fact that all the windows in the house are kept tightly shut.

Perhaps if someone can persuade the National Park Service to have a more open mind about the world of the paranormal, we will be able to determine whether it is old Abe, Mary, Edward, or all three who haunt the Lincoln home. Until that time, visitors to the home will just have to try to figure out the mystery for themselves.

Abraham Lincoln Tomb

SPRINGFIELD

ABRAHAM LINCOLN'S LEGACY CASTS A LONG SHADOW over America, but it is most noticeable in Illinois. In a state where auto license plates bear the phrase "Land of Lincoln," it is fitting that not only Lincoln's shadow but also perhaps his very ghost still walks the Illinois prairie. It is said that the sixteenth president's ghost roams the old capitol building in Vandalia; his house on Eighth Street and the Old State Capitol, both in Springfield; and, as one might expect, his tomb in Springfield's Oak Ridge Cemetery. An interesting aside here is that Lincoln's ghost also haunts the White House and possibly other sites in Washington, DC, as well as historic sites in Kentucky, where he spent his childhood. The question that ghosthunters often ask, and that remains unanswered, is how a ghost can haunt so many different places simultaneously. Lincoln must have a really good ghost secretary.

On the night of April 14 1865, Good Friday, the famed actor John Wilkes Booth fired a single bullet at point-blank range into the head of Abraham Lincoln as he sat watching a performance of the comedy *Our American Cousin* at Ford's Theatre in Washington, DC. Within a few hours the president "belonged to the ages," as Secretary of War Edwin Stanton said. In light of the many reports about Lincoln's ghost over the years since his murder, Stanton's words take on an entirely new meaning.

Lincoln himself was no stranger to the world of the paranormal. A gloomy, often depressed man, Lincoln evinced a strong spiritual side whose exact nature scholars have endlessly debated. He suffered the untimely deaths of two of his sons, Eddie and Willie, the latter being the more tragic since Willie was probably the closest of all four sons to his father and died in the White House during the upheaval of the Civil War. Willie's death ultimately drove Mary Todd Lincoln into deep depression and an obsession with spiritualism; she spent many years trying to contact Willie, and later her deceased husband, through Spiritualist mediums. It remains unclear to what extent Lincoln shared his wife's belief in Spiritualism but in any case, he was surrounded by it. The spiritual side of Lincoln's character has also been revealed through his own premonitions about death, including the time he saw two reflections of himself in a mirror, one hale and hearty, the other pale and sickly; and his dream, only a few days before the assassination, of his own body lying in state in the East Room of the White House.

Lincoln's body was embalmed, a practice that had only recently become commonplace in America in response to the need for preserving the bodies of thousands of slain soldiers being shipped home from Civil War battlefronts for burial. Mrs. Lincoln did not want her husband to be buried in Washington, DC and had the body transported back to their hometown of Springfield for interment at

Oak Ridge Cemetery. Following a funeral service in the White House, the body was brought to the Capitol, where it lay in state for public viewing. Two days later, Lincoln's body was loaded onto a special funeral train that carried the Lincoln family, close friends, and a military escort. The body of his favorite son, Willie, was removed from its vault in Oak Hill Cemetery in Georgetown and accompanied Lincoln to the Springfield cemetery. Over the next twelve days the train made a circuitous 1,700 mile trip from Washington north to New England, then west through New York and the Midwest, stopping at ten cities along the route, each time placing Lincoln's body on view in some public building. Thousands of mourners paid their last respects to the fallen president at these viewings. The train finally reached the Springfield depot on May 3.

Oak Ridge Cemetery had been built only a few years before Lincoln's death and at the time of his funeral there on May 4, 1865, the isolated cemetery was still mostly woods. Lincoln's body, along with those of Willie and Eddie, who had been exhumed from his previous burial location, were placed into a receiving vault until construction on the tomb itself could be completed. Before sealing the vault, a group of Lincoln's friends made a final check on the body to determine its condition. They hired a plumber to cut open a small section of the lead box in which the body lay. Satisfied that all was well, the box was resealed.

The ghost stories began almost immediately. As construction continued on the tomb, some people reported seeing a tall, shadowy figure inspecting the grounds late at night. People who saw the apparition had no doubt that it was Lincoln.

By 1871, the tomb had been completed enough that the three bodies could be transferred from the receiving vault to the crypts in the new catacomb beneath the tomb. Sadly, another Lincoln had already been placed in the tomb: his son Tad, who had died earlier that year from tuberculosis. Now only one son, Robert Todd Lincoln, survived. Before sealing the body of Lincoln in its crypt, however, Robert Lincoln, along with the same six friends and the plumber, once again opened the coffin to check the body. At that time they replaced the outer wooden coffin, which was rotting away, with an iron one, placing the lead box containing the body inside it. Then the crypt was sealed.

It wasn't long before people reported sobbing and the echoes of invisible footsteps coming from the tomb. For many, the ghost of Lincoln still walked.

It has been said that ghosts frequently appear in places where the dead do not lie easily, where their eternal rest is disturbed for some reason. If this is so, there can be no doubt that Lincoln's ghost walks the tomb, since his rest was so often violated; between his death in 1865 and 1901, Lincoln's coffin was moved seventeen times at Oak Ridge and opened five times, each time in the presence of his son, Robert. In 1874, Lincoln's body was moved into a new marble sarcophagus, but then, in 1876, thieves broke into the tomb and were nearly successful in stealing the president's body. The thieves were actually a ring of counterfeiters who intended to hold Lincoln's body for a $200,000 ransom and the release of their jailed master engraver. Had it not been for the Pinkerton detective who had managed to infiltrate the group and thwart their plan at the last minute, they would have been successful. With fears of another body-snatching attempt fresh in their minds, members of the Lincoln National Monument Association took it upon themselves to safeguard the president's remains. In secret, and under the direction of Robert Lincoln, they removed the casket from its sarcophagus and hid it in the passages below the tomb, hoping to rebury it. But the work was slow and interrupted by visitors to the tomb, so the casket was simply covered with boards left over from construction. Incredibly, for the next two years, Lincoln's casket lay beneath the woodpile while visitors mourned at the empty sarcophagus.

Obviously, such a sad state of affairs could not continue. As more people began to visit the tomb and workers were now on site installing some of the statuary that adorns the tomb, officials knew the body could easily be discovered. It needed to be protected much better. A group of these men organized themselves into the Lincoln Guard of Honor and, as their first order of business, began to dig a new secret grave in the tomb for Lincoln's body. This was completed in 1877 while mourners continued to pay their respects to the empty crypt.

Lincoln's body was moved again in 1886, this time to a new brick-and-mortar crypt. Before sealing the casket inside, however, it was opened and the body identified by friends. Then it was buried finally for all eternity, which lasted until 1899, when the State of Illinois decided to build a new memorial as the original one was settling unevenly and cracks were developing in it. The new memorial was completed and included a state-of-the-art burglar alarm, but Robert Lincoln was still not satisfied that his father's body would be protected from grave robbers. In 1901, under security plans that Robert had drawn up himself, his father's casket was placed in a sarcophagus ten feet below the marble floor of the tomb inside a cage of iron bars, and the hole was filled with concrete. Since that time, Lincoln's body has remained undisturbed.

But that doesn't mean that his ghost is yet at rest. Stories continue to this day of crying and whispers echoing in the halls, of footsteps and odd tapping.

The day I visited Lincoln's tomb, there was only one other visitor there. This surprised me. I thought that surely there would always be a line of visitors at the tomb, especially on a day as bright and sunny as the one I had chosen for my visit.

The tomb is immense and is immediately recognizable as one enters the cemetery. The obelisk standing over the tomb soars 117 feet, an obvious landmark. I spoke with two female guides in the round reception room of the tomb and asked them what ghostly events they had experienced. I was not surprised when they ignored my questions entirely, and chose to answer questions I hadn't asked, such as how tall was the obelisk, or how many tons of brick and mortar had gone into the construction of the tomb. Boring stuff. I had first encountered this tight-lipped response at the Lincoln home. It seemed as though those associated with the Lincoln heritage in an official capacity simply would not talk about ghost stories, or even acknowledge they existed. The stories, I mean.

I walked through the corridor to the semi-circular burial vault in

Lincoln crypt

which Lincoln's memorial, a huge red-marble stone, rested. There was no other inscription for this great man other than "Abraham Lincoln, 1809 – 1865." The United States flag stood directly behind it. To either side of the flag were two groupings of state flags. One group consisted of the state flags of Massachusetts, New Jersey, Pennsylvania, and Virginia, the states where Lincoln's ancestors had resided. The flags of the states in which Abraham Lincoln had lived—Kentucky, Indiana, and Illinois—were represented in the second group. The presidential flag stood to the right of the marker. The lighting was subdued, a single soft spotlight illuminating the stone, reflecting warmly on the cream-colored marble walls. On the opposite wall were the crypts of Mary Todd Lincoln and their sons Eddie, Willie, and Tad; Robert Lincoln was buried in Arlington National Cemetery after his death in 1926 at the age of eighty-two. As a Civil War veteran, Robert was entitled to such a burial, but it seemed that the real reason he was interred in Arlington was because Robert's widow wanted to honor the memory of her husband and his own achievements in life separately from those of his father.

There are some conspiracy aficionados who maintain that Lincoln's body is not where it's supposed to be, that it still lies somewhere else, hidden forever, while visitors remain fooled by an empty grave. But those believers are few and far between these days. No, it seems certain that Lincoln's body lies deep beneath the red-marble stone. What is far less certain is where his spirit resides.

Vachel Lindsay Home

SPRINGFIELD

THERE IS AN INSCRIPTION FROM THE VACHEL Lindsay poem "The Dream of All the Springfield Writers," written on a piece of artwork painted by a local student and hanging on the wall of the guest bedroom in the Lindsay house at 603 South Fifth Street. The inscription reads:

"I'll haunt this town, though gone the maids and men,
The darling few, my friends and loves today.
My ghost returns, bearing a great sword-pen ..."

Despite the inscription from this poem and the fact that Lindsay, the "Vagabond Poet," was born and died in the house, it is not haunted. That is, at least, the official position of Jenny Battles, the curator of the Lindsay Home, and indeed, I could find no clues to the existence of ghosts in the house as I did my research.

So why am I including the Lindsay Home in this book?

There are two reasons. First, the house that Lindsay called his "heart's home," his "spiritual center," had been the site of personal tragedies in his life, the kind that are typically associated with haunted houses. Second, no one has yet performed a formal paranormal investigation of the house to see whether or not there is any psychic energy there. While I am not saying that the house is haunted, I am saying that if ever a house existed with the potential of being haunted, it is the Lindsay house. I have often wondered exactly what it takes for one house to become haunted while another remains free of spirits, and I do think that the Lindsay Home would make an interesting test subject in this regard.

It was an overcast and wet day in November when I pulled up before the two-story, gray house. The house overlooks the Governor's Mansion from its place on a street that has seen better days, although the house itself has been restored and is in excellent condition. I parked the car and walked up the steps to the porch. Dead leaves still clung to the vines that wrapped themselves around the slim columns of the porch. A large white banner bearing an outline sketch of the poet fluttered between two of them.

Jenny Battles answered the door when I rang the bell and admitted me into the front hall. Jenny was of retirement age and wore a long skirt with a white blouse, reminding me of a Victorian librarian, and she quickly demonstrated to me the vast knowledge of her subject, typical of just such a librarian. Actually a former teacher, Jenny had a great appreciation for the art and poetry of Vachel Lindsay, having taught his work to her many students, and spoke about him with such reverence it was almost as if he were present in the room, ready to take his place on stage. But no, Jenny said, no ghosts.

The house was built in 1846 for Ann Smith, Mary Todd Lincoln's sister, and there was no doubt that Abraham Lincoln had been a visitor there. An inauguration party was held in the parlor for the Lincolns just before they left for Washington, DC, and it is believed that Lincoln spent his last night in Springfield in the house. In 1878 the poet's father, Dr. Vachel Thomas Lindsay, purchased the house. Nicholas Vachel Lindsay was born at the house on November 10, 1879, the second of six children and the only son.

When Lindsay was still a young boy, three of his sisters, Isabel, Esther, and Eudora, died within three weeks of each other in a scarlet fever epidemic. This tragedy was very hard on the family, especially since the girls' father-physician was unable to save them. Vachel became close to his remaining sibling, Olive, and maintained that closeness throughout his life. The last Lindsay child, Joy, was born when Vachel was ten years old.

The Lindsays expanded the house with an addition to the rear while leaving the front of the house mostly intact. As we walked through the rooms, Jenny pointed out the different woodwork in the two sections; golden oak simple in design in the original section, dark walnut, more intricately fashioned, in the addition. Original artwork by Lindsay's artist mother hung on the walls, as did prints of Lindsay's own art.

"Vachel always wanted to be an artist like his mother," Jenny said, "and he went to art school for formal training."

Lindsay put his art aspirations on hold, however, opting to follow his father's footsteps in medicine. "If I were an orphan, I should be an artist, but I am not so I'm going to college and be a doctor," he told a friend. When he graduated from high school in 1897, Lindsay enrolled in Hiram College in Ohio. He soon recognized that a medical profession did not suit him, however, and Lindsay was able to convince his father to let him study at the Art Institute of Chicago and later at the New York School of Art. That training allowed him to merge his art with his love of words, a passion he developed at an early age.

Most of the furnishings in the Lindsay Home are original to the family. There is a library with beautifully crafted bookcases off the dining room at the rear of the house. As Lindsay was growing up, those bookcases would have been filled with books, with the children's books set on the lower shelves.

From 1906 to 1912, Lindsay periodically went on "tramps" across the United States, logging over 2,800 miles on foot, and taking nothing with him except the clothes on his back and his poems. As strange as it may sound to our modern sensibilities, or perhaps our lack of them, Lindsay paid his way by reciting poetry or handing out copies of his poems and art, trading them for food and shelter. His reputation as a poet grew and soon he was traveling around the country, performing rather than merely reciting his poetry to sold-out crowds. His tramping exploits and his theatrical presentations made the "Vagabond Poet" a national sensation, akin to a rock star of today.

Lindsay returned to his Springfield home from time to time to visit, but just like the prophet spurned in his own homeland, Lindsay never felt that Springfield had accepted him as a poet.

In 1925, while in Spokane, Washington, the forty-six-year-old poet met a twenty-year-old schoolteacher named Elizabeth Connor. They were married only a few days later in his room at the Davenport Hotel. Four years later the couple and their two children moved to Springfield and back into the old family home.

Lindsay's childhood bedroom on the second floor became his study once the family was settled in Springfield. On my visit, a small wooden desk still stood on the painted floorboards. An old-fashioned typewriter, black and ugly, squatted upon it along with half a dozen books and two ink bottles. A bunch of flowers in a ceramic vase sat upon the desk as though Elizabeth had just arranged them for her husband. There was a single chair by the desk and a sleigh bed tucked in the corner nearby. Some school photos of the young poet hung on the wall. I remembered what Jenny had said about ghosts but it seemed to me as though Vachel had just stepped out of the room momentarily and was due to return at any moment.

Vachel Lindsay died in his home on December 5, 1931, supposedly of a heart attack, but four years later Lindsay's widow revealed the truth—the poet had taken his own life. She told the true story to poet Edgar Lee Masters, who wrote a biography of Lindsay.

According to Elizabeth, Lindsay had just returned to Springfield, exhausted from a tour on the East Coast. At one venue in Washington, DC, two hundred people in the audience inexplicably left the auditorium. Lindsay, of course, was perturbed and embarrassed by their actions. But on November 30, back in Springfield at the First Christian Church, the crowd warmed to him and treated him graciously. Lindsay remarked to a friend, "I feel that at last I have won Springfield." Still, the incident in Washington caused him pain.

In addition, Lindsay's marriage was troubled, perhaps owing to the great difference in ages between Elizabeth and Vachel, as well as the debt the Lindsays had acquired. Although he went on tour often, Lindsay realized little profit from it.

Elizabeth revealed that her husband had been emotionally unstable the last few days before his suicide, going through mood swings from melancholy to euphoria. The night of his suicide, he was distraught at dinner and he repeatedly called himself an old man whose life and work were at an end.

Sometime during the night, while Elizabeth slept upstairs, Lindsay drank down a quantity of Lysol. Elizabeth was awakened by a loud crash and found her husband lying on the floor. She helped him upstairs into bed and called the doctor, but it was too late. The poison had done its work. Lindsay expired at one o'clock in the morning.

Vachel Lindsay's spirit lives on in his poetry and art, but I can't help wondering if it doesn't also live on in the house he loved all his life, the only home he ever knew. Perhaps one of you will find the answer. If you do, be sure to let me know.

Old State Capitol

SPRINGFIELD

ON JUNE 16, 1858, ABRAHAM LINCOLN DELIVERED
his famous "House Divided" speech in Representatives Hall in the
original Illinois State Capitol building in Springfield. The speech was
made during Lincoln's campaign for the U.S. Senate against Stephen
Douglas. Lincoln lost that election, but his impassioned speech that
day focused the public spotlight upon him and only two years later he
was elected the sixteenth president of the United States.

Although a new state capitol building was constructed in 1876,
the Old State Capitol, as it is known today, is still standing, thanks

to a massive reconstruction effort in the 1960s. In the stormy years leading up to the Civil War, both Stephen Douglas and Abraham Lincoln spent much of their time in the capitol building, divided in political affiliation, but united in their efforts to preserve the union. It is impossible to tour the old capitol and not feel the presence of these men in its great chambers and halls. Some people believe that it is more than mere memory one experiences in the capitol; it may be that the ghosts of these immortal men still linger here, debating the great issues of our nation into eternity.

I visited the Old State Capitol on a cold day in December. The sun was a blurred disc in the slate-gray sky, but even in the flat light the capitol's beauty shone forth. Architect John Rague's Greek Revival building commanded a large square, enclosed by a wrought-iron fence. Four majestic stone columns supported the pediment over the main entrance. A tall and graceful cupola topped by a red dome rose from the center of the roof. An American flag proudly waved from a flagpole above it. At one point state officials had considered demolishing the deteriorating building. Luckily, wiser heads prevailed and the building was reconstructed. Each stone was dismantled, numbered, and put in storage until a new supporting structure could be built. Once that was completed, the old walls were rebuilt exactly as they had been first put up in 1837. Abraham Lincoln would recognize it immediately.

Christmas wreaths hung from the old-fashioned lampposts surrounding the square. Snow crunched beneath my boots as I walked the stone path to the main entrance. Although I hadn't seen any other people outside, there was a small group of a dozen or so individuals inside waiting to begin a guided tour of the capitol. I joined them. We stood in the spacious center hall. Before us a beautiful double staircase curved up to the second floor. Peering up through the staircase, I could see right to the inside of the dome.

Dennis was our tour guide, a personable guy with curly gray hair and wire-rimmed glasses. He was full of Lincoln lore, some of which I accepted with a grain of salt, since Lincoln himself was known to often spin a tall tale or two. We began the tour in the old Illinois Supreme Court chamber on the ground floor. As a lawyer, Lincoln was a frequent visitor to the chamber, pleading more than three hundred cases before the bench.

From there Dennis led the group into the adjacent court library and clerk's office. This room served as something of a gentleman's club in Lincoln's day; women were not allowed inside. Lincoln spent many hours here, perusing the library's collection of law books and writing his briefs. He was also a welcomed contributor to the clubby atmosphere of the room, where men played checkers and cards and swapped stories.

We followed Dennis up the elegant staircase, trimmed in fresh-cut garland, to the second floor. The capitol dome arced overhead, supported by graceful Corinthian columns. A tall Christmas tree decorated with ribbons and bows stood in the hall.

The governor's office was on this floor. Lincoln moved into the office during his 1860 campaign for the presidency. Here, he received a steady stream of well wishers, which continued for weeks after his election. Also on the second floor was the office used by Ulysses S. Grant at the start of the Civil War, before he was given a field command.

Representatives Hall, in which Lincoln served out his fourth and final term in the Illinois legislature, is perhaps the most imposing room in the building. The narrow wooden desks of the members were arranged in long semi-circular rows facing an imposing dais upon which sat the house speaker's desk. Behind the desk hung a large painting of George Washington. We walked across the red-carpeted floor, past the Corinthian columns, and stood behind the rail that separated the desks from the entrance area at the rear of the chamber.

As Dennis told us about the speeches Lincoln made in the chamber, I studied the stovepipe hat resting on the desk that had been used by Representative Lincoln. It was a rusty, black, old hat, illuminated from above by a single spotlight. The hat was a poignant reminder of the man who had been launched to fame in that very room and whose body returned to it in 1865. Lincoln's body lay in state upon the dais in that chamber, beneath the black crepe-draped portrait of

Orbs in Representatives Hall

Washington, on May 3 and 4 of that year. A crowd estimated at 75,000 filed by the assassinated president's bier to pay their last respects. On the morning of May 4, the casket was closed and removed to Oak Ridge Cemetery for burial.

I tried to imagine the open casket of the president there before me, tried to hear the muffled weeping of the people as they passed by. I remembered the sorrow and grief I felt in 1963 when President Kennedy was assassinated and remembered seeing that same grief written large on the faces of my friends and neighbors and, through the miracle of television, on the faces of the thousands of people who paid their respects to the fallen president in the capitol rotunda in Washington, DC. How tragic was that event! How tragic must it have been for those who came to that Illinois chamber in 1865, in shock that a president had been murdered. I could almost feel their grief in the air as I took photos of the chamber.

The tour ended at Representatives Hall. After most of the other people in the tour had left, I asked Dennis if he had heard of any hauntings in the capitol building. He told me that there were lots of ghost stories associated with Lincoln, but that he had never heard any connected to the building.

I wondered if perhaps Lincoln's ghost had been dislodged by the capitol's renovation. What happens to a ghost when the place it haunts is taken down, if only temporarily? Does the ghost leave for greener ghost pastures, or does it take a seat on a pile of bricks and calmly wait for the building to be rebuilt? If the building is demolished, never to be rebuilt, does the ghost continue to haunt that location, maybe finding itself trapped inside a shiny new Burger King a year later, or does it leave forever?

Back on the ground floor of the capitol, I spoke with another docent and asked him whether he knew any ghost stories about the building. He told me that he was certain the ghost of Stephen Douglas was still roaming the capitol.

"Come with me," he said. "I'll show you."

I followed him to another clerk's office. There was a little fence across the doorway so we could not enter into the room, but I could see old desks, chairs, and wooden filing cabinets, all the furnishings one would expect in a nineteenth-century office.

"Stephen Douglas haunts this room," the docent said. "See?" He pointed to a balance scale sitting upon a table across the room. "Watch it."

I did. After a few moments I noticed that the scale was slowly tipping, first to one side, then the other. Nothing else in the room moved.

Then I noticed the new air-conditioning vent high in the ceiling directly above the scale.

"That's funny," I said, trying to maintain my ghosthunter sense of humor.

"I always point it out to the school kids when they come here. Gets them every time," he said.

In the end, the joke may have been on the skeptical docent. After I downloaded the photos I had taken at the Old State Capitol onto my computer, I noticed something unusual in one photo I had taken in Representatives Hall. In the foreground was the stovepipe hat. Just to the left of it appeared a faint mist that I could not explain. Moreover, floating above the dais at the place where Lincoln's body lay in state was a single white orb—Lincoln's ghost?

South

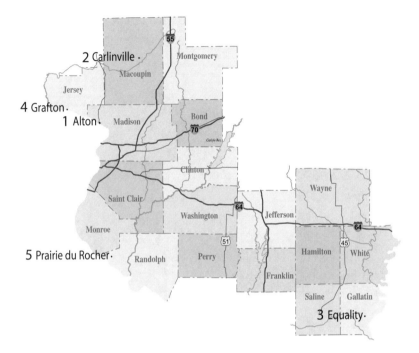

Mineral Springs Hotel
ALTON

OVER THE YEARS A LOT OF FOLKS HAVE CHECKED
into the Mineral Springs Hotel in downtown Alton. Some still haven't
checked out. I don't know if the Mineral Springs Hotel is Illinois' most
haunted hotel, but it is right up there on the short list of contenders for
the title. At least four different ghosts wander throughout the building
and there may be more. You never know.

From outside the Mineral Springs Hotel is not much to look at;
a nondescript brick building set in a nondescript brick Midwestern
downtown on the edge of the Mississippi River. The interior is every
bit as "exciting," but it wasn't always this way. When brothers August

and Herman Luer first opened the hotel in 1914, it was a showplace of extravagance, the likes of which had never before been seen in Alton and haven't since then. The Luers had first planned on building an ice house for their meatpacking business but they discovered a natural spring whose waters were considered "medicinal," because of their high mineral content, during excavation. The Luers decided to build a first-class hotel and spa instead. The interior décor of the hotel featured stained glass, decorated crown moldings and cornices, terrazzo floors, and marble staircases, all the architectural touches one would expect to see in the finest mansion.

The highlight of the Mineral Springs Hotel was the swimming pool in the basement. Elegant Grecian columns surrounded the large rectangular pool, filled with the healing waters. Used by the community as well as by hotel guests, the pool became a center for swimming lessons, water polo clubs, and even hydrotherapy sessions administered by local physicians.

A faded rose if ever there was one, the Mineral Springs Hotel had registered its last guest years before my wife, Mary, and I arrived to visit. The once opulent ground floor now contained an antique mall, a little café, and Wayne Hensley's In-Zone Barber Shop. I didn't know whom to talk to about the ghosts, but I found the management office in a corridor at the rear of the building and went inside. There I met Jerika Bateman. She told me that she had worked directly for the hotel owners, but would soon be changing jobs to conduct ghost tours and dinners at the hotel. Apparently, I had found the right person.

Although she was on her way to another appointment, Jerika was kind enough to spend some time with me and tell me about the ghosts. "You have to understand," she said, "that before I started working here, I was completely a nonbeliever when it came to ghosts. I'm a believer now."

Jerika had had more than one encounter with the hotel ghosts. She was alone in the building the first time, a day when it was closed to the public. She heard the ringing of a nonexistent bell from the area in which the front desk had been located. She distinctly heard the "ding" of the bell, as though an impatient guest was demanding service. She ignored it at first, thinking it was her imagination or perhaps the radio, but the bell rang again. And again. It rang at least four times over the next few hours, but there was never anyone there —and, of course, no bell!

After hearing strange stories from other people who had visited the hotel, Jerika permitted a psychic to do some research in the building. The psychic used a camera, an EMF (electromagnetic frequency) monitor, and a tape recorder to try to record any ghostly activity. Jerika was stunned when the psychic played back the tape and an unknown voice said, "Stop her standing there."

"By that time I guess you were convinced that there were ghosts in the hotel?" I asked.

"I was sure beginning to think so," Jerika answered. "Ghosts or something. After the psychic's visit, things got really weird."

Jerika said that she and a woman friend, a real "Bible thumper" Jerika called her, were redecorating the ladies' room on the ground floor. Suddenly they felt a cool breeze behind them and one of the stall doors opened and closed by itself. Jerika's friend was spooked and told her, "You open those doors, you let Satan in here." She was speaking metaphorically, of course, and Jerika never felt that Satan was actually using the ladies' restroom.

But if one could suppose that Satan was a guest at the hotel, then one could also make a case for the existence of angels there as well. Jerika could more than make that case. She had the photo to prove it. The hotel provides catering services for group functions and it was at one of these, a wedding in August 2003, that Jerika saw the "angel."

"I was in the downstairs ballroom, checking on things as we set up for the wedding. I had my camera with me to take pictures of the set-up. As I was taking pictures, I noticed a shape floating in the air above the tables. It was an apparition from the waist up. It looked like a cherub with curly hair and a ribbon in it. She was moving her arms. She was only there for a few seconds, but I managed to take a picture."

She showed me the picture on her computer and, sure enough, there was something there all right. It did look like an angel, although what Jerika called "arms" looked more to me like folded chicken wings.

"Was anyone else there when you saw the apparition?" I asked.

"There were a few girls working in the room at the time, but no one else saw anything," Jerika said.

Just then, Mary knocked on the door and came inside. She had been wandering around on the ground floor taking pictures while I spoke with Jerika. I introduced Mary to her. I asked if it was possible for us to tour the building, especially the basement pool.

"I have to leave now, but if you don't mind going down there on your own, I can unlock the door and let you in," she said. We gladly agreed. "Also, before you leave, you really should talk with Wayne Hensley, the barber. He's been here a long time and has a lot of stories."

Jerika led us down a set of stairs to the basement level. She unlocked a solid metal door. "Just go across that room to the door on the opposite side. The pool is beyond it," she said.

We said goodbye and opened the door. The room was pitch black. I groped along the wall for the light switch but couldn't find it. I started to walk into the room.

Mary tried to grab my arm. "Where are you going?" she said. "Watch out for the pool!"

I hesitated. "It's beyond a second door, Jerika said, didn't she?" I was hoping I had heard her correctly.

Finally, I found the light switch and flipped it on. No pool. We were standing in a whitewashed rectangular room with a dirty, faded carpet. The room was empty except for a couple of tables stacked up against a wall. On the far side of the room, three carpeted steps led up to a green metal door. A little sign on the door read: "Do not enter. Authorized personnel only. Enter only with guide."

Guide? What guide? We didn't have a guide.

I pushed the door open just a crack. Nothing but darkness beyond. I reached in, looking for the light switch, not willing to risk falling into the pool, which I assumed, was on the other side. Somewhere. Bingo, there were the lights. We went inside.

We stood on a wide, dusty concrete apron that surrounded the pool. The weak lights in the basement cast gloomy shadows in the depths of the large pool, now bone-dry and badly stained. Bits of concrete, tile, and other debris lay on the bottom. White tiles lined the walls of the pool but they were smeared with many years' worth of dirt and mold. Fluted concrete columns ringed the pool. The paint had flaked off them in large patches and a few seemed to bear scorch marks. Wires draped overhead like strange jungle vines.

A single strand of rope encircled the pool, as if that would prevent anyone from falling in, but there was also a set of wooden stairs inside the pool so visitors could walk down into it. That's what I did, walking down the sloped floor of the pool to the deep end, maybe ten or twelve feet deep. I tried to imagine what it would have been like to be swimming here in the hotel's heyday, when everything was bright and shiny and new, but I couldn't. The years had taken their toll on this place. I stood there in the depths of the pool, wrapped in a preternatural gloom, and all I could feel was a sense of melancholy and depression. Mary took a picture of me at the bottom of the pool and about all that came out was the reflective shine from my athletic shoes; that sad pool had swallowed up the rest of me.

I came up and rejoined Mary. We walked around the pool, taking pictures. The apron was littered with junk from earlier days and we were careful about where we stepped. At one end of the pool the concrete apron had totally crumbled away, leaving only a wide expanse of sand. It was almost like being on a beach, if you can imagine a beach in an ancient, sunless, moldy basement. The place got to us after a few minutes and we left. Coming back up into the light was like climbing out of an Egyptian tomb.

Back on the ground level, I stopped at the In-Zone Barber Shop to talk with Wayne Hensley while Mary explored the antique mall. The first thing I noticed in Wayne's tiny shop was the large framed portrait of *Seinfeld*'s Kramer hanging on the wall. I knew Wayne and I would get along fine.

Wayne was just finishing up with a customer, so I waited and watched him work. Wayne was tall, with short salt-and-pepper hair and a neatly trimmed moustache of the same color. He wore gray slacks and a black short-sleeved smock. When his customer had been shorn, Wayne took a few minutes to show me around.

"You've already been down to the pool?" he asked.

"Yes."

"What did you think?"

"I think it's sprung a leak," I said. "What are the stairs about?"

Wayne explained that he often conducted ghost tours through the building. He was apparently the "guide" we were warned about on the sign to the pool. "We built the stairs so that people on the tour can go down into the pool, maybe get to feel George."

"George is the ghost?"

"He's one of them," said Wayne. We had paused before the stairs to the second floor. "George never comes up from the basement and he's a bit of a flirt. Several women have seen him wearing an informal suit and heard him call them by name."

Wayne said that no one knew the ghost's real name, and I wondered why it was that unknown male ghosts in Illinois were always dubbed "George." One psychic who had been on the tour said that the ghost's name was William. William's girlfriend or wife had argued with him about something and hit him on the head, knocking him out. He fell into the pool and drowned. Another psychic said the ghost was named Robert and that his drowning was accidental, the result of a poor dive.

George, alias William, alias Robert, is not alone in the basement. A little girl ghost named Cassandra keeps him company, although she has also been known to come upstairs. Wayne told me about the time Cassandra came through during a séance in the pool.

"Everyone was standing in the pool in three circles, holding hands. We had about fifty people. We had lowered the lights, but we could see each other, so we knew that no one had broken the circles. As we stood there, a little metal marble came rolling across the floor from nowhere, but it didn't just roll. It stopped, changed direction, rolled a little, stopped again, changed direction again. Really strange. When we brought the lights up, we saw two marbles, and each of them had come to rest against the feet of two little girls who were in the group. When the group came back upstairs, some people said they saw the shadowy figure of a girl kneeling down to play marbles. It seemed that Cassandra wanted to play with the other little girls," Wayne said.

Although her name might not be accurate, Wayne said that his research revealed that a young girl had indeed drowned in the pool many years ago. On one occasion a child's bare footprint was found in the dust at the bottom of the pool. There was only the single print and it was right up against the wall, as though the child had stepped through it. Similar prints were also found on the dusty floor of one of the locked and deserted apartments upstairs.

Cassandra's artwork

Wayne was particularly moved by the story of the little ghost and conducted a test to see if he could contact her. He took a clean page from a child's coloring book, Snoopy and Woodstock sitting on the roof of the pup's doghouse, and hid it, along with some crayons, in the basement. No one else knew about his test. After several days had gone by Wayne went down to the basement to recover the page and crayons. Sure enough, purple and blue crayon was streaked all over the page. Cassandra's artwork was crude at best; she just couldn't stay in the lines, but who knows what being a ghost could do to your fine motor skills? The colored page, along with photos of orbs and mists taken in various locations in the hotel, were on view in a glass display case in the lobby.

"And then there's the Jasmine Lady," said Wayne.

The third ghost, Jasmine Lady, died on the stairs just behind us.

"She was a rich, beautiful married lady from St. Louis," Wayne said, "who was having an affair with another man. They would meet here, in one of the rooms upstairs. Her husband found out, followed her here, and confronted her. She ran from the room, but he caught up with her at the top of the stairs and gave her a push. She flew down the stairs and hit her head right here." He pointed out the steps on which her body made contact. "She broke her skull, her neck, and her cheekbones, then rolled to the bottom of the stairs, dead."

Wayne Hensley (right) and I stand at the stairs where the Jasmine Lady died

Her presence is announced by the scent of her perfume, a strong jasmine fragrance that I could detect even as Wayne spoke. I detected it even stronger in the men's room, which is at the foot of the stairs, and wondered if it wasn't the scent of disinfectant. But it's not only the Jasmine Lady's scent that remains in the hotel. People have seen her as well. One night a custodian saw a woman walking in the downstairs ballroom. He called down to her from the stairs and told her the building was closing for the day. She would have to leave. The woman ignored him and continued to walk. Right through a wall. She vanished before the custodian's eyes. He quit his job two weeks later. Thinking about the custodian's experience, I wondered if it had been the Jasmine Lady whom Jerika had captured on her photo taken in the ballroom.

The fourth ghost in the Mineral Springs Hotel is that of a young artist who had been a guest there. A typical starving artist, and something of a drunk as well, he was unable to pay his bill. To satisfy his debt, he painted a mural on a wall that is now part of the café. Like the male ghost in the basement, the artist's ghost is considered something of a ladies' man. He, too, has been known to call to women by their names and it is mostly women who have reported seeing him. Mary and I had stopped in the café earlier for lunch—grilled cheese sandwiches eaten at a table by the window—but the ghost had not bothered us.

"He's also kind of pushy," Wayne said. "He thinks the café belongs to him, maybe because of his mural, and he keeps the other ghosts out."

Right. Maybe that's why there are only four ghosts haunting the Mineral Springs Hotel.

Loomis House

CARLINVILLE

WHEN JUDGE THADDEUS LOOMIS RAN FOR REELECTION in 1865 in Macoupin County, it was understood by the electorate that a vote for him meant a vote for a brand new county courthouse and a new courthouse meant more prosperity for the little town of Carlinville. Loomis was returned to the bench and construction began on the courthouse. There was a lot of money to be made on the magnificent new building and almost immediately, the cost of construction began to spiral out of control. By the time the courthouse with its magnificent dome was completed in 1870, it had cost taxpayers more than $1.3 million, an astronomical sum in those days. Charges of graft and corruption were leveled at the judge and other members of the committee who had overseen the project. Loomis resigned from the committee in disgrace.

Controversy was focused not only on the exorbitant cost of the courthouse, but also on the fact that Judge Loomis was able to erect a luxurious new hotel on the Carlinville town square while the courthouse was being built. Where did he get the money for such a project? Was it true that the limestone taken from the courthouse project and used for the construction of the hotel was only "leftover" as Loomis claimed? Was it mere coincidence that architect E. E. Myer designed both buildings? No conclusive evidence could be found to prove that Judge Loomis had committed any crime and he was eventually cleared of any wrongdoing. But the Loomis House, as the judge's hotel was called, was born in controversy and remains controversial to this day, although for different reasons.

Ghostly reasons.

It was a tip from the Internet, a single sentence saying that Loomis House was rumored to be haunted, that had brought me to Carlinville, a town I most likely would have passed by on any other day. I parked my car in a space on the town square.

The four-story Loomis House sat on the square, across the street from a gazebo. It was a faded beauty. Only the ground floor was occupied, playing host to a bar, the House of Beauty, and Carlinville Computer Clinic. The second floor of the large building was used for storage while the top two floors, whose windows were boarded up, maintained the original hotel rooms, now lost in silent and dusty darkness.

The cold December wind whipped at me as I crossed the street to the hotel. Strings of tiny white Christmas lights framed the large windows and wrapped around the wrought-iron fence on the roof of the gallery running along the front of the building. A row of pigeons sat along the roof like miniature gargoyles. I tried the main door to the hotel but found it was locked, so I went next door to the House of Beauty. Two stylists were there but no customers.

I explained to the women why I was there. This is always a tricky proposition with people who are not expecting my visit. Their reactions could range from sticking a crucifix in my face and ordering the demon inside me to come out (or simply calling the police to escort me back to the asylum from where I had so obviously escaped) to bemused expressions of befuddlement or outright confessions of their own paranormal experiences. Luckily, it was Tammy Lewis who greeted me, and she fell into the last category.

"This place is definitely haunted," she said. "Charlotte can tell you all about it."

"Charlotte?"

"Westenberg. She and her husband, Alan, own the building. I'm not sure if she's in right now, but we can check." She led me to the rear of the shop. "I've had my own experiences here, as well," she said.

Tammy told me that she had always been sensitive to spirits and "that kind of stuff." She said that the hand of a statue she kept in the shop suddenly dropped off of its own accord and that later, a fourteen-year-old customer saw the statue hop and then fall over without anyone touching it.

"The spirits just like to mess with me," Tammy said. "One time they held down the lid of a tanning bed I was using as I tried to get out. They're real jokers."

I didn't see the joke in trying to charbroil someone, but then again, I didn't have the same familiarity with spirits as Tammy did. There was a gap in the back wall of the shop that opened up to a large area at the rear of the building. This was the computer shop. Tammy introduced me to Alan Westenberg, who ran the shop.

Alan was a smiling, hale fellow with a stocky build, in his mid to late fifties. He too, did not flinch when I told him why I was there, but deferred the ghost stories to his wife, Charlotte. She would return at any minute, he told me. While we waited, he took me on a tour of the ground floor, including a section that used to be an old apothecary and was still furnished with wonderfully detailed, hand-carved oak cabinets and display cases. Alan told me something of the history of Loomis House and why it was that ghosts might still linger there. Back in the 1870s, Loomis House had been a favorite stopping place for traveling salesmen—"drummers" as they were then called—as well as moneyed gentlemen who frequented the bar downstairs and the brothel on the fourth floor. Liquor, sex, money—all the ingredients to elevate passions and cause trouble. These were the conditions that created ghosts, and I was not at all surprised to hear Alan say that at least one murder had taken place in the building. Two drummers got into a dispute that escalated into violence on the second floor. One of the men was killed.

A few minutes later Charlotte Westenberg returned. She sported a red Christmas sweater and a cheerful nature; I had the feeling that her upbeat personality was not just a seasonal affectation, but lasted all year round. Despite the fact that the top three floors of the hotel were not open to the public, Charlotte offered to show me around the building. I could not refuse.

We climbed a narrow set of worn stairs to the second floor. The floor was a warren of rooms, large and small, most of them haphazardly filled with bureaus, armoires, dressers, mirrors, chairs, and other mismatched furniture.

"This is all my mother's stuff," Charlotte said. "She buys old furniture for our rental properties and stores it here until we need it."

As we walked through the dim rooms, we passed a flight of stairs that ran down to the street level. I could see cars pass by through the glass door at the bottom of the stairs, the door I had first tried to gain entrance into the building.

"This is the room in which the salesman was killed," Charlotte said, leading me into a small kitchen. An old '50s-style refrigerator stood against one wall. Wooden counters held coffeemakers and other assorted kitchen gadgets. A small worktable stood in the center of the room. A large cloth covered a mound of something on the table; it reminded me of a body lying under a sheet on an autopsy table. A shiver passed through me, and I didn't know if it was the chill December air leaking into the room or something else entirely that caused it.

"How did you find out about the murder?" I asked.

"We've had some psychics visit," Charlotte said. "One of them sensed the murder. A different psychic told us about Isobel. Over here," she said, and I followed her to another section where a single booth built against the wood-paneled wall held a table and two benches.

"Look at the wall. Do you see anything?"

I looked at the wall near the booth. Wood grain, knotholes, nothing exciting. Charlotte nodded her head in agreement. "Right, there's nothing there," she said, "but we have a photo taken right at this spot that clearly shows the figure of a girl or young woman standing here. Her name is Isobel."

Charlotte explained to me that a female psychic named Jenny had visited Loomis House along with some paranormal investigators. On the fourth floor of the hotel, Jenny had seen the ghost of Isobel, who warned Jenny and the researchers not to enter a certain bedroom, for fear they would be "trapped," as she had been by Judge Loomis. She said to Jenny, "I'll meet you downstairs," and sure enough, she materialized near the booth on the second floor.

According to Charlotte, Jenny has had remarkable success in finding ghosts at Loomis House. She once saw an elderly man with a black beard wearing a vest over a white shirt. Her description matched a photo of Judge Loomis. She also saw a man kneeling on the fourth floor. Jenny asked who he was and he answered, "Find me in the armoire." In the drawer of an antique armoire on the second floor, she and the researchers found some old newspapers and in one of them, a photo of a man identified as F. L. J. Breymann, a local businessman. Jenny recognized the man in the photo as the man she had seen on the fourth floor. Since Breymann's business was not located in the Loomis building, the researchers concluded that he had been one of the fourth-floor brothel's satisfied customers.

A different psychic saw the figure of a man he identified as "Parker." The name didn't mean anything to Charlotte at first, but after some investigation she discovered that a man named Parker had once been a bellhop at the hotel and would often sneak up the back stairs to visit his girlfriend on the fourth floor.

Clearly, the fourth floor was where the action had been and, apparently, was still.

The stairs up to the third floor were covered in layers of dust and scattered with debris from the crumbling walls. It was gloomy on the second floor, but by the time we arrived on the third floor, it was dark as night. There was no electricity on the top two floors and we did not carry any flashlights. I shuffled along in the darkness behind Charlotte, afraid of putting my feet down on something unseemly or perhaps finding no floor at all beneath them.

Third floor of Loomis House

"These two floors are in pretty bad shape," Charlotte said, in no way alleviating my fears. "A bad storm, a near tornado, came through here not long ago and blew out all the windows and the skylight on the roof. We had to board everything up after that."

Other than our own voices and the grating of our feet on the dirty wooden floors, there was no sound. It was as though we had gone deep below the earth, buried miles down. The silence was as palpable as a living thing. My eyes gradually became accustomed to the darkness, although not entirely. I could see that we were in a long and wide corridor, with rooms lining both sides. Most of the doors gaped open or were gone entirely, revealing only yawning black holes. In the center of the corridor a wooden rail gone fuzzy with years of accumulated dust outlined a long rectangle on the floor.

"What's that?" I asked.

"Look up," Charlotte said. Above me was a matching rectangle cut through the ceiling. I could just barely see some of the fourth-floor rooms in the darkness beyond it. "There was a large skylight set in the roof of the building," Charlotte said, "and an opening was cut into the floors of the second and third levels so that the light would reach all the way down through the building. It must have been something to see in its day. All boarded up now, except for the fourth floor."

We continued to wander the third floor, careful where we stepped. Light seeped into the building in some places, giving me a better view of the decay and destruction the years had wreaked upon the hotel. Stained wallpaper hung in curling strips from the walls. Plaster and bits of wood littered the floor. Lathing showed through in the walls like exposed ribs.

I followed Charlotte up to the fourth floor. At least I think I followed her, the darkness being so complete as to hide her from my view. I could follow only her voice.

"I really should have brought a flashlight," she said.

I crept up the stairs like a blind man on a tightrope. The air had turned noticeably cooler. I could taste the dust, smell the mold. Charlotte was somewhere ahead of me as we came out on the fourth floor, but I wasn't exactly sure where. As I stood there for a moment, getting my bearings as best I could, I heard a muffled crying.

"Pigeons," Charlotte said. "Sometimes they manage to get inside the building. Like the bats."

Great, I thought. Bats in the dark. They could see me, but I couldn't see them.

I took pictures everywhere, even though I knew that they would most likely be full of dust orbs once I downloaded them onto the computer. The flash of my camera was very strong, so I found myself using it as a sort of flashlight. I would take a picture and try to remember all the details before me, revealed only for a split second. I held my breath every time I depressed the shutter, never sure of what might suddenly be illuminated in the darkness.

We continued to explore the fourth floor. The open doorways of the guest rooms—on this floor, brothel bedrooms—were darker holes against the darkness.

"We're standing in front of Isobel's room," Charlotte said, although I could only see darkness.

I stood in the doorway, pointed my camera at what I thought was the room's interior and fired. Something seemed to jump in the room when the flash went off. Was it my own shadow? Charlotte's? Was it Isobel? The photos would reveal nothing.

The dark and dustiness, the tomblike silence of the upper floors became overwhelming and when we finally came back down to the ground floor, I felt as though I had risen from the dead.

Of all the places I visited in Illinois as I researched this book, Loomis House was the creepiest. Some investigations have already been made there, but more work is needed. Even though the upper floors of the old hotel are not officially open to the public, Charlotte will do her best to accommodate anyone who wishes to visit. Just tell her Isobel sent you.

Old Slave House

EQUALITY

THE GOOD NEWS ABOUT THE OLD SLAVE HOUSE is that it was recently sold to the State of Illinois to be preserved as a historic site. The bad news is that the state does not have the finances to renovate and operate it and so, as this book goes to press, the haunted plantation house remains closed to the public. I've included it here because there are many people working to get the house opened and, with a little luck, that may happen soon.

John Hart Crenshaw built the house, officially named Hickory Hill, in 1842 high on a windswept hill overlooking the Saline River. Crenshaw had inherited a salt mine begun by his father and by the time the younger Crenshaw built the house, he had already diversified into other businesses and holdings and was a wealthy and prosperous man, well respected by his church and the members of his community. He was also an illegal slave trader.

In the early nineteenth century, Illinois was technically a "free state," one in which slavery was illegal. There were a few instances, however, in which slavery was permissible. One such legal provision allowed slaves to be leased from Kentucky and Tennessee for a one-year period to work in the salt mines of southeastern Illinois. Working the salt mines was a backbreaking, miserable job that few free men were willing to do, so slave labor became imperative to the successful operation of the mines. Crenshaw's mines were no exception.

In the decades prior to the Civil War, thousands of escaped slaves fled northward seeking their freedom. Kindhearted people on the Underground Railroad provided safe houses for the slaves as they traveled. At the same time, there were gangs of men who made their livings by hunting down escaped slaves and returning them to their masters, or by collecting the reward on them offered by the county. These men enjoyed the protection of the law and were even allowed to continue their pursuit of escaped slaves into free states. There were some bands of slave hunters operating in Illinois along the Ohio River, and it was said that John Crenshaw had hired a few to provide workers for his mines. Of course, he also had the option of selling the captives back into slavery, a profitable sideline to his main business. Sometimes, the slave hunters would snatch up a free black, sometimes his entire family, and sell them all into slavery as "escaped slaves." It was likely that Crenshaw turned a blind eye toward such practices. In fact, Crenshaw was indicted in the late 1820s for kidnapping a free black family, but was acquitted. It was later learned that the family had, indeed, been sold to a plantation in Texas although Crenshaw could not be indicted again for the same crime.

As Hickory Hill was being constructed on Ford's Ferry Road near the town of Equality, no one would have suspected the secret architectural details that the Greek Revival–style building concealed. A tunnel linked the basement to the Saline River and provided a route by which to bring in illegal slaves. An entrance at the rear of the house was wide enough to accommodate a wagon so that slaves could be brought directly into the house, concealed from prying eyes. But the most surprising and most horrific construction was the slave prison in the third-floor attic. Here male slaves were kept chained to large metal rings in tiny cell-like rooms arranged on either side of a wide aisle as they awaited their fate. Women slaves were often subjected to the breeding room, a cell only slightly larger than the others that was home to "Uncle Bob," a large and intelligent slave who served as a stud in Crenshaw's slave-breeding business. A pregnant slave always brought a higher price on Southern auction blocks than females without children. The attic was stifling hot in the summer, cold in the winter, and illuminated only by a single window at either end of the building. There was evidence of whipping posts in the attic.

Ironically, Abraham Lincoln was a guest of Crenshaw at Hickory Hill in September 1840, spending a night there.

In 1842, Crenshaw again found himself in trouble with the law, this time accused of kidnapping a free black woman and her children, holding them in captivity for several days, then smuggling them out of state, presumably to a Southern slave market. With a lack of hard evidence, however, the prosecutor was forced to drop his case against Crenshaw. But if the law was unable to touch Crenshaw, fate was not. In 1846, some of his businesses began to decline, most notably the salt mines when other more profitable deposits were discovered in Virginia and Ohio. That same year, Crenshaw was attacked by an ax-wielding slave and lost a leg in the assault. By the time of the Civil War, Crenshaw had already moved out of Hickory Hill, leaving the house abandoned. He moved closer to Equality and died in 1871.

In 1906 the Sisk family bought Hickory Hill from a Crenshaw descendant and opened it to the public. Over the next several decades, thousands of people passed through its doors and many of them came out with stories about ghosts. It was not unusual for visitors to the attic to report cold spots and to hear strange whispers and moans in the gloomy cells. They would often feel as though someone were watching them from the empty rooms, and some even reported unseen hands and fingers touching them.

A legend grew up about the house that said no one could spend an entire night alone in the attic. It began in the late 1920s when a ghosthunter by the name of Hickman Whittington decided to try his luck at Hickory Hill. No one knows what Whittington experienced that night, but it must have been horrible. In Troy Taylor's *Haunted Illinois*, Hickory Hill owner George Sisk says that when Whittington visited, "He was in fine health but just after he left here, he took sick and he died just hours after his visit.... You might say that something scared him to death." Historian Jon Musgrave, who had spent eight years studying the Old Slave House, later discovered that Whittington did not die when Sisk said he did, but that he passed away a few years later in the state mental asylum in Anna. One can only wonder what drove poor Whittington to madness.

After that, many people tried to stay the night but were overcome by fear, including two Vietnam veteran Marines who made their attempt in 1966. Loud moaning and otherworldly voices surrounded them. Just before their kerosene lantern blew itself out, plunging the attic into total darkness, the Marines said they saw "swirling forms" taking shape in the dark. Sisk said that the men "came flying down the stairs at about one-thirty in the morning.... They were in a state of shock. They tore out of here in a hurry ... didn't even bother to go back upstairs to get their belongings."

Despite all these weird paranormal happenings, very few people have actually seen a ghost at the Old Slave House. In 1977 a college professor was touring the house alone. Although he didn't have any unusual experiences in the attic, the professor did have the unmistakable sense of some unseen presence in the room. He left the house and went outside to his car. He happened to look back at the house and there, in the attic window, was a face peering back at him. It was there for only a moment. The professor went back inside to talk to the owner of the house, who assured him that he had not gone up to the attic and that there was no one else present in the house.

Illinois psychic researcher Troy Taylor had visited the Old Slave House many times before it was closed to the public. Although he had never experienced any of the ghosts haunting the old house, he remained convinced that something unexplainable was going on in the attic. He had spoken to the last owner, George Sisk, on several occasions and Sisk also had maintained the house was haunted. Perhaps some lucky ghosthunter will be able to prove that he's right once the Old Slave House is reopened to the public.

Ruebel Hotel

GRAFTON

THE LITTLE VILLAGE OF GRAFTON, LOCATED AT the confluence of the Mississippi and Illinois Rivers, is inhabited by fewer than eight hundred souls, so when my wife, Mary, and I drove into town in our ghost-and-spook-painted Ghostmobile, we drew some attention. One interested party was the village cop who pulled us over as we drove down the main drag looking for the haunted Ruebel Hotel. We had driven that car to more than fifty haunted sites in two states, but it wasn't until we got to Grafton that an officer of the law finally interrogated us. I understood why. It was a Sunday in December, when absolutely nothing was happening in Grafton; we relieved the officer's boredom. Perhaps in the summer, when tourists were in town and the streets were busy, we would have slipped by, but not on that gray winter's day. The officer was polite enough, however, and once he was convinced we were not the advance guard of a satanic cult, he let us alone.

Just by chance, he had pulled us over directly in front of the Ruebel Hotel.

The hotel was a two-story brick building. The ground-level façade featured large windows and woodwork trimmed in burgundy and gold paint. We grabbed our bags and headed inside. Stepping into the lobby was like stepping back in time to the Victorian gaslight era. Wine-colored carpeting with pink floral wallpaper. Dark wood trim around the doors and baseboards and a wide staircase with the same wooden railings. Evergreen garland wrapped around the railings. A large Christmas tree, decorated with ribbons, bows, and lights stood in the small lobby across from the receptionist's desk. There was no one at the desk.

After a few minutes a woman came to the desk and registered us. Apparently, we were the only guests in the hotel that night so it didn't seem necessary to have someone at the desk all the time.

On the dimly lit second floor, the halls were narrow, carpeted in that same wine color. The doors to the rooms were tall, made from some dark wood, and topped by transom windows. A sofa and a few wing chairs were placed in the open area at the top of the stairs.

We didn't know who or what haunted the hotel; we had heard only that it was haunted. We thought that maybe the pervasive chill in our room could be due to a ghost but no, the desk clerk said, the hotel was always cold in the winter. She brought up a space heater for us and plugged it in.

There wasn't anything to do in the hotel and since we had been traveling most of the day, we decided on dinner. The hotel dining room was our only option. The dining room was located on the ground floor off the lobby. It was huge, considering the number of guest rooms, and sported an enormous bar at one end. Several ceiling fans hung above the tables. The decor was Wild West gone berserk. Horns, antlers, and large dead animals were mounted on the wood-paneled walls amid lariats, cowboy hats, and framed pictures of cowboys and western scenes. A framed photo of Michael Ruebel, the Bavarian immigrant who had built the hotel in 1884, hung on the wall. He wore a vest, overcoat, and round hat something like a train conductor's and looked more like der Captain from the *Katzenjammer Kids* than he did a prosperous businessman.

Even a teetotaler could appreciate the bar, a beautiful work of art with its solid, hand-carved wood and large mirrors trimmed in finely detailed wooden frames. When the 1904 World's Fair in St. Louis, Missouri, closed, Ruebel bought the bar furnishings from the Bavarian pavilion and had them shipped across the river to his saloon. Now, in place of stylishly dressed festivalgoers, two guys in hunter's camo and another one who looked liked Santa Claus bellied up to the bar.

Other than the three wise men, Mary and me, one bartender, and the waitress—who doubled as the desk clerk—there was no one else in the big room. The dark night pressed against the window near where we sat eating our dinner. The street was empty and shiny with rain. I could hear Edgar Allan Poe whispering in my head, "Once upon a midnight dreary, while I pondered, weak and weary..." It wasn't yet midnight, but those were my sentiments exactly.

When the waitress brought our bill, I asked her what she knew about the ghosts that were rumored to haunt the hotel. She really didn't know much, she said. The ghost was supposed to be that of a little girl, but she had never seen it.

I had hoped to speak with Jeff and Sandy Lorton, the owners of the Ruebel Hotel, but neither one of them was there at that time, so Mary and I retired to our room. When we got back up on the second floor, we noticed two framed prints that we had not paid attention to before. Both of them depicted a little blond girl with blue eyes.

"Is that our ghost?" I said.

"That would be nice," Mary said. "She's a cutie."

Our room had now warmed up to sauna temperatures, thanks to the space heater. We tried to read in the anemic glow provided by a single overhead light, but soon gave up and called it a night. In the darkness we heard the rain drumming upon the roof.

Then I heard what sounded like a footstep on the carpet. I was instantly alert.

"What is it?" Mary asked.

"Shhh," I said, "Listen."

There was only quiet, then the footstep again.

"Did you hear that?" I asked.

"Yes," Mary whispered.

The footstep padded on the carpet one more time.

Just like an actor in a horror film, you know whom I mean—the idiot who always has to open the closet door, even though we all know what's behind it—I jumped out of bed and scrambled for the light switch. At the same time, I felt something cold and wet touch the back of my neck. The light revealed nothing.

I stood there for a while, looking around the tiny box of a room for the person or thing that had been walking across our carpet. Mary sat up in bed watching me, certain no doubt, that she would be signing my commitment papers any day now.

Then we both heard the sound once again. Something plopped on the carpet.

"You've got to be kidding me," I said, as I studied the ceiling. A drop of water seemed to materialize out of the ceiling, dangled for a moment and then fell to the floor. After a few seconds, another drop fell. "The roof is leaking," I said.

"You don't suppose they'll charge us extra for that, do you?" Mary said.

I grabbed the wastebasket out of the bathroom and set it under the leak. The water reverberated in the room like a pistol shot as it hit the plastic can.

"I don't know, but so much noise will probably scare our ghostly pals away," I said. I called the waitress/desk clerk from our room phone and told her about the problem. She assured me that it would be taken care of as soon as the owners returned later that night. The rain abated about an hour later and the leak stopped. We had already fallen asleep and no one ever checked to see if we had drowned.

We finally met Sandy Lorton the following morning. In the hall outside our room a housekeeper was talking with a thin woman wearing a housecoat. I thought by her attire that she may have been another guest, but when the housekeeper addressed her as "Sandy," I knew better.

After introducing ourselves, we followed Sandy downstairs. As we headed to the dining room for breakfast, she told us about the ghost. "I've lived here in the hotel for eight years now," Sandy said, "and I've never seen anything. But who knows, maybe I'm just not sensitive to those kinds of things."

She told us about three women from Peoria who had stayed at the hotel and had seen a girl first in their room and then running in the hall outside their door. Sandy said that the women described the girl as being "ghostly," lacking in substance. They also said that she looked like the girl in the framed prints hanging on the wall.

"Who is the ghost girl? Does anyone know?" I asked.

"Her name is Abigail," Sandy said. "Many years ago she was passing through town with her father, when she became sick. Her father took a room here to take care of her, but she died. It's her ghost that is supposed to haunt the hotel. The ghost stories go way back before Jeff and I bought the place."

"Has anyone else seen the ghost?"

"Barb, one of my former housekeepers, swore that someone tapped her on the shoulder, but there was no one there," Sandy said. "You can talk to the rest of the staff, if you like. Maybe they'll have some stories."

After breakfast we went upstairs to pack our bags. I stopped to talk with Margarette Werner, a housekeeper who was folding linens on the couch near the stairs.

Margarette said that she had never seen the ghost either, but that she had often heard doors slam in empty rooms. She also told me about Heather, a college student who had worked in the hotel one summer but quit and never came back. The ghost had scared her away, Margarette said.

Heather was sitting on the couch by the stairs when a door to the second-floor porch suddenly blew open. Heather felt a cold draft pass by, as though a person were walking by, and also felt the sensation of someone watching her. Then she noticed the shadow of a girl in a long dress moving across the wall.

"That really frightened her," Margarette said. "She was alone in the hall. Another time she saw a girl in old-fashioned clothes standing in the hall. After that, Heather would never work up here alone and she quit soon after."

Margarette said Heather had heard that the hotel was haunted before she started working there, but that she didn't know it was haunted by a girl. Her experiences corroborated the stories that had been told for many years. "I don't know if the hotel is haunted," Margarette added, "but I do know that strange things happen here."

Pere Marquette State Park Lodge
GRAFTON

AFTER SPENDING A NIGHT AT THE HAUNTED RUEBEL Hotel in Grafton, my wife, Mary, and I were planning on leaving town, headed for new adventures in ghosthunting farther south. We had heard that the Grafton area was noted for its winter gathering of migratory birds, especially bald eagles, so we thought we would make a brief stop at Pere Marquette State Park, only a few miles down Great River Road from the hotel, to see if we could spot any interesting birds. We pulled into the visitors center and went inside. In a conversation with one of the park rangers, I casually mentioned that I was writing a book about Illinois ghosts.

"Is that why you're here?" he asked. "To chase our ghosts?"

"What? No, we came here to chase birds," I said. "You've got ghosts?"

"So they say," the ranger replied. "In the lodge."

Sometimes, this is the way it goes. The spirits just want to be helpful. We immediately drove over to the lodge and booked a room. Even if we didn't find any ghosts, we knew we would enjoy our stay at the lodge. It was magnificent.

Originally built in the 1930s by the Civilian Conservation Corps, the huge lodge is built of native stone and rustic timbers on a site that once served as a village for Hopewell and Illini Indians. There were fifty guest rooms in the lodge and twenty-two stone guest cabins. The lobby featured a mammoth stone fireplace that soared fifty feet to the roof and weighed 700 tons. Massive timbers supported the roof, and huge beams crossed the expanse overhead. Fabric artwork crafted by Joan Lintault, an art professor at the University of Southern Illinois at Carbondale, hung from the rafters. Titled *Four Rivers*, the piece was composed of four panels, each of them measuring eleven by eighteen feet. More than six thousand fabric leaves and fabric turtles, fish, birds, frogs, butterflies, snakes, dragonflies, and ticks (yes, ticks), were added to the fabric, each of them stuffed to give them dimension.

The lodge was decorated for Christmas. The lights on the twelve-foot-tall Christmas tree were reflected in the varnished wood floors. Wreaths threaded with tiny white lights hung in the large picture windows that overlooked the Illinois River.

As we had been in the Ruebel Hotel, Mary and I were alone in the lodge, with the exception of a few day guests who had come there for lunch. Ideal ghosthunting conditions, nice and quiet. But first things first. Before we did any ghosthunting, we had to try out the huge chess set in the lobby. Large wooden pieces, measuring as much as three feet high, were placed on a board approximately ten feet square. We lugged the pieces around as we made our moves and I finally won, but only because Mary had been exhausted by all the manual labor.

Mary and I had requested a room in the original section of the lodge, rather than the newer wing at the opposite end, thinking that our chances of a ghostly encounter would be increased in the older section. As Mary relaxed in the room, I wandered around the lodge.

I met Gena Hatch, the lodge's assistant general manager, and told her why I was there. She was not at all shy about telling me about her own ghostly experience. She said that she had been behind the registration desk working night audit. The registration area is located in a small reception area just before the lobby.

"It was in the wee hours and I was alone," Gena said. "Since there was no one else around, only a few lights were on in the lobby. Suddenly, I saw something cross the doorway to the lobby. I saw it only from the corner of my eye, so I couldn't identify it, but I knew it was something large. When I went out into the lobby to check, there was nothing there." The thing had never made a sound, nor was there any physical evidence of anything having been in the lobby. "I have no idea what it was," Gena said, "but it was pretty creepy."

She also told me about the housekeepers who were cleaning rooms in the old section of the lodge, the very area where my room was located. The housekeepers were cleaning the carpeting and had piled the furniture on top of the beds. Suddenly, a nightstand that was on the bed began to shake violently while everything else in the room remained calm. The women got out of there fast.

That evening, Mary and I had dinner in the lodge's restaurant. We asked our waitress if she had heard any ghost stories about the place. She said that although she had never seen him, she had heard other servers talk about an old man who was sometimes seen sitting by the fireplace, but who would disappear when approached. The ranger at the visitors center had told me that some people had seen a man wearing a Civil War uniform in the lobby. I asked our waitress if the man by the fireplace wore a uniform. She didn't know, so I wasn't sure if we were talking about one or two ghosts. It turned out that there was some rationale for a Civil War ghost since a detachment of Federal soldiers had set up a small camp on land that is now part of the park in order to protect access to the two rivers.

After dinner we walked to the new wing of the lodge, to the indoor swimming pool for a dip. It was beautiful, with one glass wall that looked out over the river, although now it looked out onto the dark winter night. Later, we made ourselves comfortable in the lobby, my ghosthunting strategy being simply to stay up late into the night to see what happened.

"This is it?" Mary said. "This is your whole plan?" Sometimes, my methods lack the planning and attention to details that my scientist wife would like.

"This is it," I said, sinking back into the soft leather upholstery of the couch and setting my feet on the coffee table before me. "This is what I do."

We were alone in the enormous lobby. We each had a book to read, although I could not concentrate and kept lifting my eyes from the page to check out the room. It was close to midnight and only a few lights were on, creating little pools of light in the expansive darkness of the vast space. The timber support columns glowed in the lamplight, but their higher sections were swallowed up in the gloom gathered above us. I could barely see the huge iron chandelier suspended there from heavy chains. A low fire was burning on the hearth across the room, its yellow flames reflected in the wood floor. The little white lights in the wreaths at the windows struggled to hold back the black night swarming against the cold glass. There was no sound to disturb us. No television, no radio, no voices, nothing. I had the uncanny feeling that I had been there before, but then I realized that I was confusing this lobby with a scene from a movie. In that dark witching hour, the lobby looked exactly like the interior of the hotel from *The Shining*. That was okay, I thought, as long as we didn't end up with Jack Nicholson taking an ax to our bedroom door.

There was actually a reason for me to stay up, however. Gena had told me that one of the housekeepers might have some stories to tell me, so I was waiting for her to come in. After sitting quietly in the lobby for a few more minutes, halfheartedly reading my book, I heard voices from the reception area. Mary curled up on the couch while I went out to the reception desk to talk with the night crew.

There were two women at the desk. Unfortunately, neither of them was the housekeeper Gena had recommended, who, it turned out, would be coming in to work in the morning. Neither of the women at the desk had any stories to tell. I woke up Mary and we turned in for the night. Sometimes ghosthunting is a lot of waiting for nothing.

The next morning I found Patty Newingham working in the new section of the lodge. She was pushing a cart through the hall, and when I stopped her and told her I was a ghosthunter writing a book about ghosts, she at first gave me that wary look that I had grown accustomed to seeing over the last two years of ghosthunting. But she warmed up shortly and repeated the story about the rocking nightstand, adding that the housekeepers called whatever had caused the movement "George."

"Why George?" I asked.

She didn't know. The name just seemed appropriate somehow, Patty said. I wouldn't be surprised if future research showed that there was someone named George associated with the lodge or the land on which the lodge was built. I've known that to happen before. Someone gets an impression of a name for a ghost and later, a real-life identity is found for that name. It's almost as if the ghost wants to be discovered and does what it can to bring about that discovery.

Patty had some other stories as well. She told me that her sister, who used to work at the lodge as a housekeeper, had met up with a ghost. Patty said that as her sister was working alone in one of the rooms in the old section, she felt someone brush up against her. Startled, she turned around. There was no one there. Another time, she felt that sensation as she was working in the lobby, again alone.

Mary and I were checking out of the lodge that day. As I was paying my bill at the front desk, I had a conversation with a young woman sitting in a chair in the reception area. Jackie hadn't worked at the lodge long, but even she had a ghost story to tell me. It had been early evening when she was working the front desk. There was no one in the reception area, but all of a sudden, the doors to the little vestibule leading outside opened wide and closed, followed by the second set of doors, which opened to the outside.

"It was really weird," Jackie said. "How could two sets of doors have opened and closed like that? It couldn't have been the wind, either, since the doors were opened from the inside."

I walked over to the doors and checked them. The first set had a bar that you had to push down in order to open the door; the wind couldn't have done that. Also, those doors were heavy to push open. Any wind strong enough to have opened the doors would have caused some havoc in the reception area. But where would such a gust of wind have come from in the first place? I couldn't figure it out.

Many questions about the lodge remain unanswered. I'd like to go back to Pere Marquette State Park some day, not just to take in all that peaceful beauty again, but also to see if perhaps George the ghost might be willing to answer a few of those questions.

Fort de Chartres

PRAIRIE DU ROCHER

THE LITTLE HAMLET OF PRAIRIE DU ROCHER IN southwest Illinois is easily missed. Despite the fact that it was one of the earliest French settlements along the Mississippi River, growth and prosperity have somehow bypassed the place and you will not casually stumble across the town; you have to be looking for it. You know you are close when you see road signs for the "larger" towns that surround it, places like Kidd, Modoc, New Design, Red Bud, and Ruma.

Prairie du Rocher retains much of its original eighteenth-century appearance, when French settlers moved in alongside a Native American village and built Saint Anne's Church and the first Fort de

Chartres. There are still a few homes in the little town constructed in the old French style, and wooden or metal crosses mark the village cemetery's ancient graves in the French tradition. There is a large aluminum cross by the cemetery that designates the site of the original St. Joseph's Church, which began as a mission outpost of St. Anne's at Fort de Chartres. A historical marker reads in part: "Here lie buried the remains of Michigamea Indians, early French adventurers, black slaves, victims of wars, massacres, floods and plagues. Veterans of all wars of the United States and pastors and parishioners of St. Joseph Church of three centuries—May they rest with God."

My wife, Mary, and I drove into Prairie du Rocher on a sunny and sleepy Sunday. We had come from the central plains of Illinois, and so the great change in topography as we headed south was unexpected. There were no more flatlands. On narrow country roads we wound through wooded hillsides and bluffs, up and down hills, before entering the village. A handful of little houses clustered beside the road, surrounded by trees and steep slopes. The village looked more like small-town Vermont than it did Illinois. A yellow dog crossed the road ahead of us and a flock of turkey vultures described lazy circles in the blue sky. These were the only signs of life in the village.

We drove through the village, descended the bluffs overlooking the Mississippi River and picked up the road to Fort de Chartres. Less than five miles from the village we saw the walls of the fort rising from the grassy bottomlands along the river. Mary is not much of a military history buff and, since we had been on the road for some time and it was a warm and sunny day, she opted for a nap on a bench in a small picnic area outside the fort while I visited the structure.

I walked the winding gravel path to the fort. The limestone walls of Fort de Chartres spread out before me, a bastion at either end overlooking the shallow dry moat surrounding the fort. An impressive main gate, surmounted by the French coat-of-arms, rose from the center of the wall. Its huge wooden doors stood open. In the silence of this rural environment, with nothing but the fort in sight for miles around, it was easy to imagine what it would have been like in 1760 when the stone fort, replacing earlier wooden forts, was finally constructed. Illini, Kaskasia, and other Native Americans would have been seen here trading furs and pelts for European goods. Rough-and-tumble French voyageurs visited the fort from time to time, trading their own wares, remaining long enough to swap stories with the blue-coated soldiers of the French Colonial Infantry who garrisoned the fort. These people were long gone, but it seemed to me as though their spirits still remained.

I was surprised to find, once I passed through the gate, that the fort had been only partially restored. Whereas the eastern wall, through which I had just passed, contained the two bastions, musket ports, and embrasures for cannon, the opposite wall and half of the sidewalls of the fort were missing. I discovered that the only building original to the 1760 fort was the powder magazine, which is believed to be the oldest building in all of Illinois. Everything else had been reconstructed, although on the original site and to the eighteenth-century dimensions. The square fort was small, enclosing about four acres and, in its day, would have been home to only about three hundred soldiers. Two stone structures at the rear of the fort held the Piethman Museum, which contained artifacts relative to the fort's early history, and the guards building, which included the guards' house, officers' room, gunners' room, priest's room, and a chapel. Other structures, such as the barracks and government house, were "ghosted," that is, not fully restored but outlined in structural timbers to give visitors a sense of their original size and form.

The reconstruction of the fort was something of a miracle. In the 1763 Treaty of Paris that ended the Seven Years War between France and England, most of France's North American colonies were ceded to the British, including the settlements in the Illinois Country. On October 10, 1765, only five years after the fort had been constructed, British troops of the 42nd Royal Highland Regiment took possession of Fort de Chartres. But the erosion caused by the Mississippi River and the elements proved to be strong foes and in 1771, the British abandoned the fort. A year later, the south wall and its bastions collapsed into the river. By 1820, trees were growing in the walls and what was left of the deteriorating buildings. Local villagers carried off much of the stone for their own use. By 1900 none of the walls existed above ground level and all of the buildings, except for the powder magazine, had vanished completely. In 1913, the Illinois state legislature began restoration efforts, most of which were carried out in the 1930s by the Works Progress Administration.

I wandered around inside the fort. There were no other visitors. The door to the powder magazine stood open and I stepped inside. Wooden powder casks were stacked three rows high along either side of a narrow aisle beneath the barrel-vaulted ceiling. Each of them was stamped with the French fleur-de-lis. A small window at the opposite end admitted dim light. I stood there for a few moments, trying to absorb whatever energy I could from the one original building at the fort, but I couldn't detect anything unusual. No surprise there, I thought, since the ghost story I had heard about the fort had nothing to do with the powder magazine.

But I was surprised when I walked out of the magazine and saw in the distance, three men in eighteenth-century coats and tri-corner hats, armed with muskets. I stepped around another building to get a better view and momentarily lost sight of the men. When I was again in a clear spot to see them, they had vanished. Ghosts? It seemed too easy, I thought.

I walked to the rear of the fort, toward the guards' building near where I had last seen the men. As I approached, a man stepped out of the building. Definitely not a ghost, the young man wore a dark suit and had a white boutonniere attached to his lapel. Another older man, similarly attired, followed him. They waved to someone off to my right and when I followed their gaze, I saw a woman in a fancy gown walking from a parking lot that I had not noticed before alongside the fort. It took me only a second to realize that a wedding was about to take place at the fort.

I walked behind the guards' building, and there were my ghosts. Two of the ghosts were smoking and talking about a Chicago Bears football game while the third was pushing a ramrod down the barrel of his musket. The ghosts' Jeep was parked just a few yards away. Apparently, these "ghosts" were re-enactors, who, along with the four women in eighteenth-century dresses, aprons, and caps who were cooking something in a large iron pot inside the guards' building, would all be part of the wedding.

I did not see any ghosts that day at Fort de Chartres, but stories of their existence persist. One of the most intriguing stories concerns the phantom funeral procession, which has been seen making its mournful way along the road leading from the fort to the cemetery in Prairie du Rocher. The first recorded visitation by the ghostly train was on July 4, 1889. That night, two women who were sitting on the porch of a house along the road suddenly noticed a large group of people coming up the road. The women were curious about the group since it was almost midnight and there were never many people out and about in the little village at that time of night. As the group drew closer, the women saw as many as forty wagons, along with carriages, horsemen, and men and women walking. The women noticed that one of the wagons carried a casket, which roused their curiosity further—why would a funeral be held at midnight? And how could it be that the parade was entirely silent? No horses' hoof beats. No wagon wheels turning. No footsteps of the passing people. Not a sound, except for the barking of a dog, owned by one of the women, that obviously was agitated by the silent procession. The barking dog woke up the woman's husband, asleep in their house next door. He looked out the window and also witnessed the ghostly cortege. After a while, the procession passed by and disappeared in the darkness. Although the women waited up for it, the procession never returned.

No one knows who the ghosts are or why they walk in a funeral march, but Troy Taylor, in *Haunted Illinois*, offers two possible explanations. One story says that an important man in the area had gotten into an argument with an officer at the fort and was accidentally killed during their disagreement. The commander of the fort decided to cover up the man's death and ordered a secret burial at midnight in the cemetery outside Prairie du Rocher. A similar story has two officers, one French, the other British, arguing over the affections of a local girl in 1756, ending in swordplay and the death of the British officer. The Frenchman fled the area, and the Englishman was buried secretly to prevent the incident from causing larger hostilities between the two nations. Unfortunately, neither story can be documented, so the true nature of the ghostly funeral procession remains a mystery.

It is said that the procession returns every time July 4 falls on a Friday. The next time that will happen is in 2014. You have plenty of time to make your travel plans.

Afterword

IN THE LAST TWO YEARS I HAVE VISITED ALMOST seventy haunted sites in Illinois and Ohio. At each of them I have tried to find some quiet time to perform my own investigation, free of the influences and biases of other people. In addition to my own experiences and observations, I interviewed the people who have had paranormal events happen to them at these places. In each chapter of both *Ghosthunting Illinois* and *Ghosthunting Ohio* I wed the two approaches to give my reader an overall impression about the haunted location. I write in an objective, journalistic style and leave it to my readers, especially those who actually visit the places in my books, to decide for themselves if a particular location is haunted or not.

As I talk about ghosts at libraries, bookstores, and community centers, or in interviews with magazine, newspaper, radio, and television reporters, one question is invariably raised: Do you believe in ghosts?

What should matter for my readers, I think, is not so much what I believe as what the many people I have interviewed believe. There is no doubt in my mind that these people absolutely believe that what they saw, or heard, or felt cannot be explained in any rational, logical way. They are convinced that their experiences can only be explained as a brush with the paranormal, with ghosts. Who am I to tell them otherwise? These people live or work or regularly visit the places and know them intimately. They have spent more time at these places than I ever did and are thus in a much better position to experience ghostly phenomena. Ghosts don't necessarily appear on demand, and it would be a rare occurrence for one to make itself known during a single investigation. Not impossible, but rare. Other ghosthunters have told me about repeatedly investigating a site purported to be haunted and spending hours there, photographing the place, taking tape recordings and noting various types of measurements, only to find nothing that conclusively proved the existence of a ghost. In short, I took my interviewees at their words, and so should my readers.

It may seem as though I am looking for an easy way out of the question, Do you believe in ghosts? Maybe I am. When my editor, Jack Heffron, asked me to write these books, he did so because he respected my abilities as a writer, not because he thought I was an accomplished ghosthunter. Indeed, before doing the research for these books I had no ghosthunting experience at all, nor can I honestly say that I spent a whole lot of time thinking about ghosts. That's all changed. The last two years have certainly made me a ghosthunter, perhaps not in the intensive style exhibited by ghosthunter clubs and "professional" ghosthunters, but a ghosthunter nonetheless. While writing my books, I have read entire library shelves of other ghost books and have developed working relationships with many authorities in the paranormal field. It is also safe to say that my thoughts in the last two years have been largely focused on ghosts and have been directed toward that all-encompassing question of belief in them. Still, I consider myself the "average Joe" when it comes to ghosts, and I have the feeling that my beliefs may match those of many of my readers.

Do you believe in ghosts?

At the risk of sounding like I am taking a cop-out, I cannot answer the question with a simple "no," nor can I answer with an unqualified "yes." There, I hope that was helpful.

It may be more helpful to rephrase the question to, Do ghosts exist? If we can prove the existence of ghosts, we would then have to believe in them, whether we see them or not, right? I've never seen oxygen or radio waves, but I believe in them, science having proven their existence to me. I'm still not sure about computers, though, which I suspect may be a form of black magic. Possibly the work of fairies.

All right, so can we prove that ghosts exist? In truth we may never be able to do so, but at the same time, no one can prove that they do not exist. Perhaps we can at least explore some theories that might allow for the possibility of ghosts.

I have no idea whether Albert Einstein believed in ghosts, but some of his theories in the realm of physics may support their existence. Einstein proved that all the energy of the universe is constant and that it can neither be created nor destroyed. Energy can be transformed, however, from one type of energy into another, a process that takes place all the time. Further, Einstein proved that everything is made up of energy. Even a seemingly solid sheet of steel is composed of an invisible latticework of madly swirling atoms generating energy. The human body is no less a mass of energy produced by the billions upon billions of atoms that make up its corporeal reality. So what happens to that energy when we die? If it cannot be destroyed, it must then, according to Dr. Einstein, be transformed into another form of energy. What is that new energy? What does it look like? The being that used to be me is broken down into its raw components, energy "leaking" out in the various states of decomposition as pure elements. But is that all that happens? What of the energy that composed our spirit, our spiritual essence? What happens to that?

Consider the possibility that the energy of that spiritual essence continues on in some way, or is transformed to a state of energy that does not require a corporeal state. Could we call that new creation a ghost? Most psychic researchers are convinced that ghosts are beings of pure energy. They document a ghostly presence by fluctuations in electromagnetic frequency as recorded on electromagnetic frequency meters (EMFs). Some researchers believe that ghosts, creatures of energy themselves, feed off other energy sources to "live," thus explaining the blown fuses, exploded light bulbs, and dead batteries that occur on so many paranormal investigations.

A second theory of physics, courtesy once again of Dr. Einstein, may offer us another clue as to whether ghosts exist. Einstein proved that light moves at a speed of 186,000 miles per second, or 700 million miles an hour. To give you an idea how fast that is, the distance from the earth to the moon is about 239,000 miles. Nothing can move faster than the speed of light. Another strange effect of the speed of light, one that I won't even pretend to understand, is that time slows down as an object or person accelerates toward the speed of light. We've all seen the sci-fi movies or *Twilight Zone* dramas in which a space traveler blasts off from earth and returns many years later to find his wife has grown old and died and his children are senior citizens while he has hardly aged a day since he departed. Can this amazing phenomena somehow support the existence of ghosts?

All right, strap yourselves in while I try to explain. It's going to be a bumpy ride.

Could it be possible that some of that spiritual essence I talked about, once it is freed from the body as energy, approaches speeds that come close to the speed of light? If that is so, then the energy would be slowed down, in a sense held back in time and space. Further, if that energy still retains its spiritual nature, then would that not mean that there would exist some spiritual being still bound in our realm, a being we might call a ghost? Wouldn't this theory of a slowed-down being unable to escape earthly bonds also provide an explanation for why ghosts are often seen over many years before finally disappearing?

Or, do I just need to sit down and get a grip?

Physics alone may not provide an answer for the question of whether ghosts exist. But there are other areas we can study that may be helpful. Religion and the various views of an afterlife held by different faiths offer intriguing avenues of inquiry.

Almost every religious creed maintains some belief in an afterlife, a realm after death in which the dead person's spirit lives on. For Christianity and some other faiths, the type of afterlife reserved for the spirit depends upon the type of life the person lived on earth. Thus, in Christianity at least, a good person's spirit is rewarded in Heaven; a bad person's spirit is punished in Hell. The essential point here, however, is not about reward or punishment but is about the basic assumption that the spirit lives on after death. No Christian would question that.

Christian theology is full of references to spirits, and here the distinction should be drawn between spirits and ghosts. Spirits, such as angels and demons, are discarnate beings that never had a human existence. Ghosts, on the other hand, are discarnate beings who were at one time human. Catholic theology, at least, rejects ghosts and communication with the dead, yet stories of miraculous appearances to the living made by the Virgin Mary, as well as many other saints, abound. The New Testament itself describes how Jesus suddenly appeared to the apostles on the road to Emmaus after his death and in the sealed and shuttered upstairs room as well. At the risk of being burned at the stake as a heretic, may I say that all these appearances seem, well, ghostly? They are certainly similar in content and detail to contemporary ghost stories.

Members of other faiths also assume the spirit lives on after death.

Hindus believe that the spirit is reborn again after death in another body, the process known as reincarnation. In Hindu belief, the soul or spirit of the deceased person hovers near the body for a time in a liminal state of ghosthood. Funerary rites over the next several days involve food and water offerings in order to rebuild a "body" in which the spirit may traverse the world of the living on its way to return to the ancestors, and eventually become reborn.

Buddhists, too, believe the spirit is repeatedly reincarnated until it finally attains enlightenment, nirvana, and is freed from the cyclical process. There is also a time of ghosthood in Buddhist philosophy. According to their beliefs, there are eight stages of death. In the final stage of death, the spirit separates from the body but does not immediately become reincarnated. The person's spirit is not even aware that the person has died and may try to speak to or interact with living friends and family. The spirit is confused but can travel anywhere instantaneously without obstruction. Further, it maintains its five senses, even though it has no physical body. This state of ghosthood is said to last no more than forty-nine days. During those days the living relatives of the dead person offer prayers that the spirit may find a good person into which it will be reborn.

The Spiritualist Church bases its entire theology upon the belief that each one of us lives after death and that our spirits may be contacted by the living to offer advice, guidance, comfort, and support. Ghosts are an accepted fact among Spiritualists and are not to be feared. An elderly Spiritualist minister I met during my research told me that she had grown up with ghosts, saw them all the time, and was thoroughly accustomed to communicating with them. She had no fear of them, telling me that she feared the living far more than any ghost.

It is entirely possible, of course, that the accumulated wisdom of countless generations from all around the world regarding a belief in some kind of life after death is just plain wrong. A skeptic could say that such a belief is invented simply to help us cope with the chilling idea that life comes to an abrupt end at the grave, that without such a belief, life would be worthless and without meaning.

These people are not invited to parties.

The religious beliefs and traditional tales of billions of people of various cultures worldwide seem to allow for the possibility that ghosts do exist. Combined with some of the laws of physics mentioned earlier, we might say that the possibility is made stronger. But can we prove beyond a shadow of a doubt that ghosts exist?

No.

While I do believe that, as Einstein proved, the energy that is "I" goes on in some unfathomable way after death, I don't have the words to articulate what that means. I am also embarrassed to admit that I do not have the imagination to conceive what existence would be like after death.

I think back on the many interviews I conducted while doing my research and find that they offer few clues as to whether ghosts truly exist and, if so, what such an existence means. I have heard stories about ghosts who repeatedly blow out candles on restaurant tables or rearrange the place settings after a server has set them down, and I think that surely there must be a better way to serve out eternity. Or footsteps up and down the stairs all night long, every night. Or rolling a pool cue ball across the floor. I'm sorry, but I fail to see much of a plan to such an afterlife, nor do I have much interest in participating. And I think once you've walked through a door without opening it, that's it. You've done it all.

I can't help but wonder if these various physical manifestations ascribed to ghosts are not something else entirely. Thousands of years ago, early man felt the earth tremble and quake, saw it split open before his very eyes, and believed those actions to be caused by angry gods, rather than sliding tectonic plates. Ancient Chinese saw the sun disappear from the sky and believed that a dragon had swallowed it.

I can listen to my favorite golden oldies station and, even though I can't see them or explain them, I believe that radio waves are bringing me those tunes. What I'm saying is that, smug as we may be due to our incredible twenty-first-century knowledge and technology, we are still learning, we are still developing technology. It may be that the weird and sometimes frightful actions we attribute to ghosts may be simply the palpable manifestations of some scientific principles we do not yet understand. Perhaps a new scientific discipline, ghostology, will emerge that will attach ghostly activities to rational and logical sources. The mystery of ghosts, and the thrill of chasing them, will be gone.

But what if science fails to explain them away, as it has failed to do thus far? That will keep you and me busy, won't it?

Ghosthunting
Travel Guide

AMERICA'S
HAUNTED
ROADTRIP

Visiting Haunted Sites

EACH OF THE HAUNTED LOCATIONS IN THIS BOOK is placed into one of four Illinois geographical regions: Metro Chicago, North, Central, and South. In most regions it is possible to explore multiple locations in a few days or a weekend. Some regions may require a week or more if you plan on visiting every location. In all cases it is a good idea to call ahead to each of the places you wish to visit to make sure they will be open when you want to go.

Happy ghosthunting!

METRO CHICAGO

It would stand to reason that in a city as historic and populous as Chicago there would be many haunted locations. This grouping contains sites that are found in downtown Chicago (other sites in the greater Chicago area can be found in the North Illinois section). You can easily explore these sites in a few days or a weekend.

❧ **Beverly Unitarian Church** (773) 233-7080
10244 South Longwood Drive, Chicago, IL 60643
www.buc.org

The Beverly Unitarian Church holds a Sunday service at 10:30 a.m. While the Unitarians welcome anyone to their services, please remember that the building is a place of worship and should be treated with respect.

❧ **Biograph Theater** (773) 549-0500
2433 North Lincoln Avenue, Chicago, IL 60614

The Biograph Theater is a working theater, although it no longer shows the Clark Gable films that John Dillinger enjoyed. Call ahead to see what's playing and, after the show, step across the street for a nightcap at the haunted Red Lion Pub. Just don't trip over Dillinger's ghost on your way out.

❧ **Excalibur** (312) 266-1944
632 North Dearborn Street, Chicago, IL 60610

Originally built in 1892 as the home of the Chicago Historical Society, the Romanesque-style brick building now houses Excalibur, a popular nightclub. If you can see through your dance partner, you know you've met one of Excalibur's resident ghosts.

❧ Glessner House (312) 326-1480
1800 South Prairie Avenue, Chicago, IL 60616
www.glessnerhouse.org

The Glessner House is located in the Prairie Avenue Historical District, an area of renovated historic homes and new upscale housing. Some of Chicago's wealthiest families—Armour, Fields, Kimball, Pullman--called this neighborhood home. Today, you can walk the area streets and witness its revival for yourself.
    HOURS: Hourly tours at 1 p.m., 2 p.m., 3 p.m. Wednesday – Sunday. $10 admission fee; free on Wednesday.

❧ Graceland Cemetery (773) 525-1105
4001 North Clark Street, Chicago, IL 60613
www.gracelandcemetery.org

The beautiful Graceland Cemetery was established in 1860 and since that time has received many of Chicago's most illustrious citizens. Their final resting sites are marked by elegant examples of Victorian funerary architecture set among curving lanes and large shade trees. And, of course, there are the ghosts.
    HOURS: Daily from 8 a.m. – 4:30 p.m.

❧ Harpo Studios (312) 633-1000
1058 West Washington Boulevard, Chicago, IL 60607

I don't know if Oprah Winfrey believes in ghosts, but many people say that Harpo Studios, where her television program is produced, is haunted. The studio incorporates the original 2nd Regiment Armory building, which served as a makeshift morgue for the 844 victims of the 1915 Eastland disaster.

❧ Jane Addams Hull-House Museum (312) 413-5353
800 South Halsted Street, Chicago, IL 60607
www.uic.edu/jaddams/hull/hull_house.html

Located on the campus of the University of Illinois at Chicago, the Hull-House museum preserves the history and artifacts pertaining to the settlement house established by Jane Addams to aid Chicago's poor immigrants. Although much of what was formerly the settlement house is long gone, the museum is located in the original building. Make sure your guide shows you the film about the history of Hull House and lets you view the settlement dining hall in the adjacent building.
    HOURS: Tuesday – Friday, 10 a.m. – 4 p.m.; Sunday, noon – 4 p.m. Free admission.

❧ Museum of Science and Industry (773) 684-1414
57th Street and Lake Shore Drive, Chicago, IL 60637
www.msichicago.org

Even if there were no ghosts this would be a museum you should not miss when in Chicago. The Burlington Zephyr, the recreated coal mine, the U-505 submarine, the 3,500-square-foot model train layout, the more than 200 authentic human specimens in the Body Works exhibit, are just part of the many treasures the museum has to offer. The museum is located in a beautiful park setting along Lake Michigan and offers plenty of parking in its underground garage. It just doesn't get any better than that.
HOURS: Monday – Saturday, 9:30 a.m. – 4 p.m.; Sunday, 11 a.m. – 4 p.m. Closed Christmas. Adults - $9, seniors - $7.50, children - $5.

❧ Red Lion Pub (773) 348-2695
2446 North Lincoln Avenue, Chicago, IL 60614
www.theredlionpub.com

Stop in at this North Side pub for a taste of authentic English fare. You may be lucky enough to share space at the bar with one of the pub's ghosts.

NORTH ILLINOIS

This section lists haunted places in the greater Chicago area and in other parts of northern Illinois. Visiting these sites will take you through some of the older suburban areas around Chicago, but will also have you traveling west across the prairie to the rolling hills and bluffs along the Mississippi River. Haunted cemeteries, restaurants, and historic sites can all be found in this region.

❧ Bachelor's Grove Cemetery
143rd Street, east of Ridgeland Avenue, Midlothian, IL 60445

This cemetery lies in the Rubio Woods Preserve and is not maintained. Ghosthunters should be aware that the cemetery is in poor condition and lacks security. It may be difficult to find the road into the cemetery, especially in the summer when the surrounding woods are in full leaf. The best access is to park your car in the Rubio Woods parking lot on the north side of 143rd Street. Two cell towers are visible across the street. Cross the street and go to the right of the towers. You should then come across the road to the cemetery. The cemetery is less than a quarter-mile down the road. Don't worry about cars; a chain bars the road, which hasn't seen vehicular traffic in many years.

» **Country House Restaurant** (630) 325-1444
241 55th Street, Clarendon Hills, IL 60514
www.burgerone.com

Casual dining in a rustic atmosphere has made The Country House Restaurant a
Chicagoland favorite for over twenty-five years. It's home to the "Country Burger,"
recently voted "Chicago's Favorite Burger" by the readers of *The Chicago Tribune*, and
it's also home to a few well-fed ghosts.
HOURS: Monday, 11 a.m. – 11 p.m. (kitchen), 11 a.m. – 1 a.m. (bar).
Tuesday – Thursday, 11 a.m. – 12 a.m. (kitchen), 11 a.m. – 1 a.m. (bar).
Friday and Saturday, 11 a.m. – 1 a.m. (kitchen), 11 a.m. – 2 a.m. (bar).
Sunday, noon – 11 p.m. (kitchen), noon – 1 a.m. (bar).

» **DeSoto House Hotel** (815) 777-0090
230 South Main Street, Galena, IL 61036
www.desotohouse.com

The DeSoto House Hotel has been welcoming guests and ghosts since 1855. It is
located in the heart of historic downtown Galena, and its comfortable rooms and
fine restaurant make it a great place to stay while ghosthunting in the area.

» **Galena/Jo Daviess County Historical Society and Museum** (815) 777-9129
211 South Bench Street, Galena, IL 61036
www.galenahistorymuseum.org

In addition to having its own resident ghosts the Galena History Museum provides
visitors with an intriguing look back at the spirit of Galena. It's a small museum but
very well done and should not be missed when visiting the town. A gift shop off the
lobby has an excellent collection of books about Galena and Illinois, as well as other
interesting items.
HOURS: Daily, 9 a.m. – 4:30 p.m. Closed on Easter, Thanksgiving, Christmas Eve/
Day, and New Year's Eve/Day. Adults - $4, Ages 10-18 - $3. Children under ten free.

» **Turner Hall** (815) 777-3020
115 South Bench Street, Galena, IL 61036
www.turnerhall.com

Turner Hall is owned by the City of Galena and may be rented for a variety of events
(there is no charge for the ghosts). Over the years, Turner Hall saw many famous
visitors and speakers, including William McKinley and Teddy Roosevelt. Although it
is not open to the public on a regular basis, visitors can call the number above to see
when the hall is open.

⋊ **Mount Carmel Cemetery** (708) 449-8300
1400 South Wolf Road, Hillside, IL 60162

Mount Carmel Cemetery is the final resting place for the "Italian Bride," Julia Buc-
cola Peta , as well as many of Chicago's 1920s gangsters such as Al Capone and Frank
Nitti.
HOURS: Daily, May – Aug., 8:30 a.m. – 7 p.m., Sept. – April, 8:30 a.m. – 5 p.m.

⋊ **Widow McCleary's Pub & Grill** (708) 877-7011
400 East Margaret Street, Thornton, IL 60476

Have a beer at Widow McCleary's, one of Al Capone's Prohibition-era breweries. Play
with the little girl ghost in the upstairs poolroom.
HOURS: Monday – Thursday, 11 a.m. – 10 p.m. (kitchen), 11 a.m. – 1 a.m. (bar).
Friday and Saturday, 11 a.m. – 12 a.m. (kitchen), 11 a.m. – 2 a.m. (bar).
Sunday, 12 p.m. – 10 p.m. (kitchen), 12 p.m. – 12 a.m. (bar).

OTHER PLACES OF INTEREST

⋊ **Annie Wiggins Guest House** (815) 777-0336
1004 Park Avenue, Galena, IL 61036
www.anniewiggins.com

Owned by Wendy and Bill Heiken, the Annie Wiggins Guest House is a comfortable
bed and breakfast established in an elegant Victorian-era mansion. This is a great
place for ghosthunters to stay while visiting Galena, since Wendy is knowledgeable
about local hauntings and conducts ghost tours of the city.

CENTRAL ILLINOIS

Central Illinois is truly the Land of Lincoln. His legend casts a long
shadow over the cities and towns scattered across the prairies. The
Illinois capitol, Springfield, is located in this region, as are other cities
such as Bloomington, Decatur, and Peoria. Ghosthunters could spend
a weekend or more visiting haunted locations in Springfield, but should
allow at least a week to include sites in the neighboring cities.

⋊ **Pumpernickel's Deli & Eatery** (309) 820-1200
113 North Center, Bloomington, IL 61701
www.pumpernickels.net

Pumpernickel's is located in the center of downtown Bloomington in a fine old building constructed in 1856. Stop in for one of the restaurant's signature deli sandwiches or soups and maybe you'll meet the resident ghost.

HOURS: Monday, 10 a.m. – 4 p.m., Tuesday – Thursday, 10 a.m. – 8 p.m. Friday and Saturday, 10 a.m. – 8 p.m.

⋫ C. H. Moore Homestead (217) 935-6066
219 East Woodlawn Street, Clinton, IL 61727
www.chmoorehomestead.org

The C. H. Moore Homestead is located one block east of Business Route 51 at the north edge of Clinton, which is roughly halfway between Bloomington and Decatur. The homestead is a beautiful Victorian mansion listed on the National Register of Historic Places. In addition to the fine furnishings, the mansion also contains the DeWitt County Museum in the basement. Site manager Larry Buss knows everything there is to know about local history, and he's always glad to share it with visitors.

HOURS: The homestead and museum is open from April–December. Tuesday–Saturday, 10 a.m. – 5 p.m., Sunday, 1 p.m. – 5 p.m. Free Admission.

⋫ Greenwood Cemetery (217) 422-6563
606 South Church Street, Decatur, IL 62522

The main entrance to Greenwood Cemetery is at the very end of South Church St. Ghosthunters can also get a view of the hillsides at the rear of the cemetery where ghost lights have been seen by taking 51 South and exiting right onto Lincoln Park Road. Park in the lot on the right.

HOURS: Daily from sunrise to sunset.

⋫ Meyer Jacobs Theatre, Hartmann Center for the Performing Arts
Bradley University (309) 677-2651
1501 West Bradley Avenue, Peoria, IL 61625

Ghosthunters who take in a theatrical performance at the Meyer Jacobs Theatre may be lucky enough to catch a glimpse of the Lady in Brown. Call ahead to find out what's playing.

⋫ Peoria Public Library (309) 497-2000
107 N. E. Monroe Street, Peoria, IL 61602
www.peoria.lib.il.us

The library is in downtown Peoria and is a great place to spend some time, whether you run into a ghost or not. If you don't, you can always check out some ghost books.

HOURS: Monday – Thursday, 9 a.m. – 9 p.m., Friday and Saturday, 9 a.m. – 6 p.m. Closed on Saturdays Memorial Day through Labor Day.

❧ Dana-Thomas House (217) 782-6776
301 East Lawrence Avenue, Springfield, IL 62703
www.dana-thomas.org

The Dana-Thomas House is in a quiet residential section of central Springfield and is only a stone's throw from the Old State House and other historic sites. A good time to visit the house is during the Christmas season, when it is decorated for the holidays. One hour tours are available with a introductory video.
HOURS: Wednesday – Sunday, 9 a.m. – 4 p.m. Suggested donation of $3/Adult, $1/Child.

❧ The Inn at 835 (217) 523-4466
835 South Second Street, Springfield, IL 62704
www.innat835.com

What better place for a ghosthunter to lay his or her weary head than at the haunted and beautiful Inn at 835? It's conveniently located in the center of the city, close to many other historic sites, some of them haunted. Innkeeper Court Conn can direct you.

❧ Abraham Lincoln Home (217) 492-4241
426 South Seventh Street, Springfield, IL 62701

The Lincoln Home looks exactly as the Lincolns left it when they departed Springfield in 1861, heading for Washington, D.C. Period furnishings recreate the everyday life of the family. Several blocks of reconstructed buildings surround the house, giving the visitor the sense of stepping back in time to Lincoln's day.
HOURS: Daily, 8:30 a.m. – 5 p.m. Closed Thanksgiving, Christmas, and New Year's days. Free admission, although there is a fee for the Seventh Street lot.

❧ Abraham Lincoln Tomb, Oak Ridge Cemetery (217) 782-2717
1441 Monument Avenue, Springfield, IL 62702

Oak Ridge Cemetery is located at the end of Monument Avenue. It's easy to find since there is plenty of street signage marking the way. It's impossible to miss the tomb once you've entered Oak Ridge. Follow the signs to the parking lot and walk a hundred yards or so to the tomb.
HOURS: Daily, March – Oct., 9 a.m. – 5 p.m.; daily, Nov. – Feb., 9 a.m. – 4 p.m. Closed New Year's, Thanksgiving, and Christmas days.

» **Vachel Lindsay Home** (217) 524-0901
603 South Fifth Street, Springfield, IL 62701

There have been no ghost sightings (yet) at the Vachel Lindsay Home; maybe you'll be the first ghosthunter to make that claim. But ghost or no ghost, the house is an interesting tribute to the memory of America's "Vagabond Poet," who was born and died there.

HOURS: The Vachel Lindsay Home is open for guided tours Tuesday – Saturday from noon to 4 p.m.. The tour is free, but donations are welcomed.

» **Old State Capitol** (217) 785-7960 or (217) 785-7961
Fifth and Adams Streets, Springfield, IL 62701

The Old State Capitol is easily accessed from either Fifth or Sixth Street. Its red dome is a distinctive landmark. An underground parking garage is below the capitol. After touring the capitol building, it's a short walk to the Lincoln-Herndon Law Offices and the Illinois State Historical Library.

HOURS: Tuesday – Saturday, March – October, 9 a.m. – 5 p.m.; Tuesda y – Saturday, November – February, 9 a.m. – 4 p.m. Closed New Year's, Thanksgiving, and Christmas days. The last tour begins thirty minutes before closing. There is a suggested donation of $2/adult and $1/child.

OTHER PLACES OF INTEREST

» **Museum of Funeral Customs** (217) 544-3480
1440 Monument Avenue, Springfield, IL 62702
www.funeralmuseum.org

The Museum of Funeral Customs is located just outside the gates of Oak Ridge Cemetery on Monument Avenue. It is dedicated to the history of American funeral and mourning customs, funerary art, and practice. The museum contains fascinating exhibits, including a recreation of a 1920s embalming room, a horse-drawn hearse, a reproduction of Abraham Lincoln's casket, and many other interesting displays.

HOURS: Tuesday – Saturday, 10 a.m. – 4 p.m., Sunday, 1 p.m. – 4 p.m. Closed Mondays and holidays. Admission is $3/Adult, $2/Senior, $1.50/Child (6-17), Free for children 5 and under.

SOUTH ILLINOIS

This region is nothing at all like the rest of Illinois. Flat prairies give way to rolling hills along the Ohio, Mississippi, and Wabash Rivers. Populated mostly with small towns, southern Illinois is the "nature" region, much of it covered by the Shawnee National Forest. A hunter's and fisherman's paradise, the region remains largely unchanged from when French explorers and Native Americans roamed the land. It's no surprise that ghosts still roam this region as well.

❧ **Mineral Springs Hotel** (618) 462-4247
301 East Broadway, Alton, IL 62002

The Mineral Springs Hotel now contains an antique mall, café, and the In-Zone Barber Shop, owned by ghost tour guide Wayne Hensley. Stop in and check the place out for yourself or book a tour with Wayne.

❧ **Loomis House Hotel** (217) 854-4458
118 East Side Square, Carlinville, IL 62626

Charlotte and Alan Westenberg and their family own the Loomis House Hotel, which is no longer a hotel, but houses various businesses. Although the top three floors of the old hotel are closed, Charlotte will arrange a tour if you call her ahead of time. She can be reached at the phone number above.

❧ **Old Slave House**
Ford's Ferry Road, Equality, IL 62934

At the time this book was on its way to the publisher, the Old Slave House was still closed to the public due to lack of funds to renovate and open it. The State of Illinois, however, has every intention of eventually opening the house so ghosthunters should keep abreast of the situation.

❧ **Ruebel Hotel** (618) 786-2315
217 East Main Street, Grafton, IL 62037
www.ruebelhotel.com

Things are pretty quiet in Grafton in the winter, so ghosthunters may want to take that fact into consideration when planning a hunt. The quieter it is, the better to experience ghosts. Winter is also the best time to view eagles along the river.

❧ **Pere Marquette State Park Lodge** (618) 786-3323
Route 100, P.O. Box 158, Grafton, IL 62037
http://dnr.state.il.us

The haunted lodge is located in Pere Marquette State Park, located in a bend in the Illinois River. Camping, hiking, cycling, horseback riding, bird watching, swimming, boating, and fishing are all available at the park and lodge. The lodge also has a full restaurant and gift shop. Summer is peak time at the park, so keep that in mind as you are making your lodge reservations.

❧ Fort de Chartres (618) 284-7230
RR 2, Prairie du Rocher, IL 62277

Fort de Chartres is located on the banks of the Mississippi River in the tiny hamlet of Prairie du Rocher, one of the original eighteenth-century French settlements. The partly reconstructed fort contains the Piethman Museum and various events are held there throughout the year. The two-day rendevous, held the first weekend in June, features shooting competitions, military drills, dancing, music, food, and traders of eighteenth-century-style goods. Fort Kaskaskia and the Pierre Menard Home are just a few miles downriver from Fort de Chartres. Traveling north from the fort on SR 3 will take you to the historic sites of Cahokia, including the plaster and timber Church of the Holy Family, which was built in 1799, making it the oldest church west of the Allegheny Mountains.

HOURS: Tuesday – Saturday, 9 a.m. – 5 p.m. Closed New Year's, Thanksgiving, and Christmas.

OTHER PLACES OF INTEREST

❧ History and Hauntings Book Co. (618) 465-1084
515 East Third Street, Alton, IL 62002
www.historyandhauntings.com

This unique bookstore specializes in two things, history and hauntings. The store boasts a wide selection of books on those topics relative both to Illinois and beyond.

HOURS: Monday – Friday, 10 a.m. – 5 p.m., Saturday, 10 a.m. – 3 p.m.

Ghostly Resources

WEB SITES

All About Ghosts
www.allaboutghosts.com

This site covers ghostly events throughout the U.S. and features ghost stories, photos, and a state-by-state index of haunted locations.

Alton Haunted Tours
www.altonhauntedtours.com

This is the official site for Jerika Bateman's motor coach tours of haunted Alton.

Annie Wiggins Ghost Tour
www.ghostsofgalena.com

Wendy Heiken is "Annie Wiggins" as she conducts a ghost tour of haunted locations in Galena. She and her husband Bill also operate the Annie Wiggins Guest House, a great place to stay while ghosthunting in Galena.

Ghost Research Society
www.ghostresearch.org

Dale Kaczmarek's site has reports about investigations conducted by the Ghost Research Society as well as information about ghost tours in the Chicago area.

Ghost Village
www.ghostvillage.com

Ghost Village says it's the "Web's largest and most comprehensive supernatural community." No doubt. There are plenty of true ghost stories and discussions here.

History and Hauntings
www.prairieghosts.com

Troy Taylor's Web site contains ghost stories, information on tours and paranormal events, as well as access to Whitechapel Productions, a publisher of paranormal books.

International Ghost Hunters Society
www.ghostweb.com

The IGHS was founded by Drs. Dave Oester and Sharon Gill. Their Web site has more than nine thousand photos, a newsletter, and also offers a home-study course to become a Certified Ghost Hunter.

Museum of Funeral Customs
www.funeralmuseum.org

The Web site for Springfield's Museum of Funeral Customs has pertinent information about the museum as well as some interesting photos.

Richard T. Crowe
www.ghosttours.com

For several years Richard Crowe has provided ghost tours in the Chicago area. The Web site has full details and the latest schedule of tours.

Sangamon Valley Ghost Research Group
www.svgrg.com

This is home to the Sangamon Valley Ghost Research Group, psychic investigators working primarily in the central Illinois area.

The Shadowlands Ghosts & Hauntings
http://theshadowlands.net/ghost/

Over 7,400 true ghost stories are collected on this site, which covers all of the U.S.

Springfield Ghost Society
www.springfieldghostsociety.com

This site describes the activities of one of Illinois' better-known psychic research groups, the Springfield Ghost Society.

Will County Ghost Hunters Society
www.aghostpage.com

This is the site for a new ghosthunting group formed in 2004. The site contains information on many haunted Illinois sites, as well as ghost stories, photos, and research information. The group can also be contacted to conduct paranormal investigations.

FURTHER READING

Bonansinga, Jay.
The Sinking of the Eastland. Citadel, 2004.

Guiley, Rosemary Ellen.
The Encyclopedia of Ghosts and Spirits. New York: Checkmark Books, 2000.

Holzer, Hans.
Ghosts. New York: Black Dog and Leventhal, 2004.

Kachuba, John B.
Ghosthunting Ohio. Cincinnati: Emmis Books, 2004.

Kaczmarek, Dale.
Windy City Ghosts. Alton: Whitechapel Productions, 2000.
Windy City Ghosts II. Alton: Whitechapel Productions, 2001.

Musgrave, Jon.
Slaves, Salt, Sex and Mr. Crenshaw. IllinoisHistory.com, 2004.

Rich, Jason.
The Everything Ghost Book. Avon: Adams Media Corporation, 2001.

Steiger, Brad.
Real Ghosts, Restless Spirits, and Haunted Places. Canton: Visible Ink Press, 2003.

Taylor, Troy.
Haunted Chicago. Alton: Whitechapel Productions, 2002.
Haunted Illinois. Alton: Whitechapel Productions, 2001

Watson, Daryl.
Ghosts of Galena. Galena: Gear House Incorporated, 1995.

Books of Interest

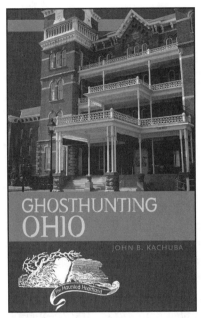

Ghosthunting Ohio

By John Kachuba

Ghosthunting Ohio examines more than thirty of the spookiest haunts all over the Buckeye State, from cemeteries to inns and taverns to libraries and cafes.

Follow Kachuba from the safety of your armchair as he explores each eerie location, brushing aside cobwebs and peering into dark rooms. Or, if the "spirit" moves you, check the Travel Guide at the back of the book for all the information you need to visit each site on your own. Either way, you'll experience goose bumps at:

- The Majestic Theatre in Chillicothe, where Army victims of the 1918 Spanish Influenza epidemic were "stacked like cordwood"
- Fort Meigs in Perrysburg, where an invisible soldier has been known to walk employees to their cars at night
- The Cincinnati Art Museum, home to at least three ghosts—including that of a seven-foot-tall medieval monk
- Twenty-nine other hair-raising locations around Ohio.

Kachuba documents these phenomena with the curious yet skeptical eye of a "Regular Joe." In the afterword, renowned psychic researchers Ed and Lorraine Warren offer their alternative ghostly theories—as well as advice on becoming an enlightened ghosthunter yourself.

Paperback Price $14.99
ISBN: 1-57860-181-9

Books of Interest

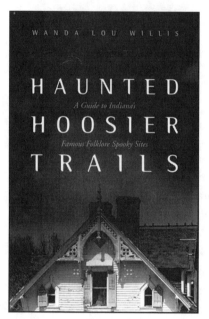

Haunted Hoosier Trails
A Guide to Indiana's Famous Folklore Spooky Sites

By Wanda Lou Willis

When European settlers first arrived in what would become Indiana, the Miami, Delaware, and Potawatomi Indians who lived in the region already had a long tradition of stories about tragic deaths and restless spirits. Over time, the pioneers, farmers, and later, city dwellers gathered their own stories about ghosts, apparitions, and voices from beyond the grave. In *Haunted Hoosier Trails*, folklorist Wanda Lou Willis passes on these local legends, along with modern folk tales that will raise the hair on your head and stoke the fires of your imagination.

Journey with Wanda Lou Willis to Hazelcot, the deserted dream mansion in Whitley County, Indiana; to the forsaken tomb of the riverboat captain along the Ohio River, where to this day boats toot out their homage to avoid the ghost's curse; and to the bridges near Avon, Indiana, where the unexpected happens around Halloween. Do ghosts walk the trails, back roads, highways, and byways of the Hoosier Heartland? Find out for yourself!

Paperback Price $15.95
ISBN: 1-57860-115-0

Books of Interest

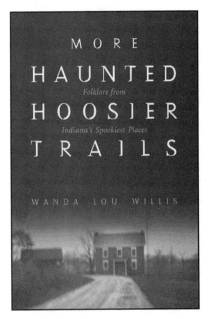

More Haunted Hoosier Trails
Folklore from Indiana's Spookiest Places

By Wanda Lou Willis

Beloved Indiana folklorist Wanda Lou Willis returns with an all-new collection of hair-raising tales about spooky cemeteries, lonely roads and haunted homes all over Indiana. Local history buffs will relish the informative county histories that begin each chapter, while thrill-and-chill-seekers will eagerly search out these frightening locales.

In *More Haunted Hoosier Trails*, you can:

- Park your car along Moody Road in Jasper County to find the tell-tale lantern light of a remorseful young man who accidentally decapitated his brother.
- Get a lesson in fear at Indiana University in Bloomington, long believed to be among the most haunted campuses in the country.
- Learn about strange happenings and restless spirits in cities, towns and counties all across the state.

The carefully researched and truly scary tales by one of Indiana's most respected folklorists will enthrall even the most skeptical reader. *More Haunted Hoosier Trails* is a terrifyingly good read.

Paperback Price $14.99
ISBN: 1-57860-182-7